# TABLE OF CONTENTS


Introduction . . . . . . . . 2
Temperature Probe . . . . . . . . 4
Defrosting . . . . . . . . 6
Defrosting Frozen Convenience Foods . . . . . . . . 9
Heating Canned Food and Leftovers . . . . . . . . 10
Frozen Convenience Foods . . . . . . . . 11
Appetizers . . . . . . . . 12
Candies and Cookies . . . . . . . . 14
Eggs and Cheese . . . . . . . . 15
Fish and Seafood . . . . . . . . 17
Fruits . . . . . . . . 20
Meats . . . . . . . . 21
Pasta, Rice and Cereal . . . . . . . . 30
Pies . . . . . . . . 32
Poultry . . . . . . . . 33
Sauces . . . . . . . . 38
Soups . . . . . . . . 39
Vegetables . . . . . . . . 41
Quick Breads and Cakes . . . . . . . . 45
Microwave Shortcuts . . . . . . . . 48


## POWER SELECT SETTINGS*

Your microwave oven is equipped with six power select settings and **DEFROST**. This variety of settings offers you flexibility in microwave cooking. Listed below is the approximate percentage of cooking power and approximate wattage at each power setting.

| Power | Output |
|---|---|
| HIGH | (700 watts/full power) |
| MEDIUM | (490 watts/70% power) |
| MEDIUM-LOW | (370 watts/55% power) |
| DEFROST | (245 watts/35% power) |
| LOW | (210 watts/30% power) |
| WARM | (70 watts/10% power) |

****Note:*** *Only applies to units with touch control panels.*

## COOKING WITH MICROWAVE ENERGY

Microwaves are a form of high frequency electromagnetic waves similar to those used by a radio. Electricity is converted into microwave energy by the magnetron tube. The microwaves travel from the magnetron tube to the oven cavity where they are reflected, transmitted or absorbed.

### Reflection

Microwaves are reflected by metal similar to the way a ball would bounce off a wall. Most metal cookware and utensils are not recommended for microwave cooking since they would produce uneven cooking. Also, if a metal dish is placed close to the oven wall, (which is also metal) arcing (bluish sparks) could occur. Arcing can damage an oven or cause a fire.

### Transmission

Microwaves pass through some materials such as paper, glass and plastic much like sunlight shining through a window. Because these substances do not absorb or reflect the microwave energy, they are ideal materials for microwave cooking containers. However, they will get hot during cooking, because as food cooks, heat is conducted from the food to the dish.

### Absorption

Microwaves are absorbed by food. They penetrate to a depth of about 3/4 to 1 1/2 inches. Microwave energy excites the molecules in the food (especially water, fat and sugar molecules), and causes them to vibrate very quickly. The vibration causes friction and heat is produced. In large foods, the heat which is produced by friction is conducted to the center to finish cooking the food.

## FOOD CHARACTERISTICS AND THEIR EFFECTS ON MICROWAVE COOKING

### Bone and Fat

Both bone and fat affect cooking. Bones may cause irregular cooking. Meat next to the tips of bones may overcook while meat positioned under a large bone, such as a ham bone would be undercooked. Large amounts of fat absorb microwave energy and the meat next to these areas may overcook.

### Density

Porous, airy foods such as breads, cakes or rolls take less time to cook than heavy, dense foods such as potatoes and roasts.

### Quantity

Two potatoes take longer to cook than one potato. As the quantity of the food increases so does the cooking time.

### Shape

Uniform sizes heat more evenly. The thin ends of a drumstick will cook more quickly than the meaty end. To compensate for irregular shapes, place thin parts toward the center of the dish and thick pieces toward the edge.

### Size

Thin pieces cook more quickly than thick pieces.

### Starting Temperature

Foods that are room temperature take less time to cook than if they were refrigerator temperature or frozen.

## PRECAUTIONS TO AVOID POSSIBLE EXPOSURE TO EXCESSIVE MICROWAVE ENERGY

(a) Do not attempt to operate this oven with the door open since open-door operation can result in harmful exposure to microwave energy. It is important not to defeat or tamper with the safety interlocks.

(b) Do not place any object between the oven front face and the door, or allow soil or cleaner redsidue to accumulate on sealing surfaces.

(c) Do not operate the oven if it is damaged. It is particularly important that the oven door close properly and that there is no damage to the:
(1) door (bent)
(2) hinges and latches (broken or loosened)
(3) door seals and sealing surfaces

(d) The oven should not be adjusted or repaired by anyone except properly qualified service personnel.

## COOKWARE AND UTENSIL GUIDE

| ITEM | USE | COMMENTS |
|---|---|---|
| Aluminum Foil | Shielding | Small strips of foil can be molded around thin parts of meat or poultry to prevent overcooking. Arcing can occur if foil is too close to oven wall. |
| Browning Dish | Searing Meats | Check browning dish information for instructions and heating chart. Do not preheat for more than 8 minutes. |
| Brown Paper Bags | None | May cause a fire in oven. |
| Dinnerware<br>Microwave Safe, only | Reheating and Short Term Cooking | Check manufacturers' use and care directions for suitability for microwave heating. Some dinnerware may state on the back of the dish, ''Oven-Microwave Proof''. |
| Disposable Polyester Paperboard Dishes | Cooking | Some frozen foods are packaged in these pans. Can be purchased in grocery stores. |
| Fast Food Carton with Metal Handle | None | May cause arcing |
| Frozen Dinner Tray<br>Metal<br>Plastic | Reheating<br>Reheating | Frozen dinners may be heated in foil tray, if tray is less than ¾-inch high. Place foil tray in center of oven. Leave at least 1-inch space between foil tray and oven walls. Heat only 1 foil tray in the oven at a time. For containers more than ¾-inch deep, remove food and place in a similar size microwave-safe container. |
| Glass Jars | warming | Remove lid. Heat food until just warm. Most glass jars are not heat resistant. |
| Glassware<br>Heat Resistant Oven Glassware and Ceramic, only | Cooking | Ideal for microwave cooking. May have many pieces available in your home. |
| Metal Twist Ties | None | They may cause arcing and could cause a fire in the oven. |
| Oven Cooking Bag | Cooking | Follow manufacturer's directions. Close bag with the nylon tie provided, a strip cut from the end of the bag, or a piece of cotton string. Do not close with metal twist tie. Make six ½-inch slits by closure. |
| Paper Plates and Cups | Reheating and Short Term Cooking | Use to warm cooked foods, and cook foods that require short cooking times such as frankfurters. |
| Paper Towels and Napkins | Reheating and Cooking | Use to warm rolls and sandwiches. |
| Plastic<br>Microwave Safe, only<br>Cookware and Storage Dishes | Cooking | Should be labeled, ''Suitable for microwave heating''. Check manufacturer's directions for recommended uses. Some microwave safe plastic dishes are not suitable for cooking foods with high fat content. |
| Plastic Wrap | Cooking | Use to cover foods during cooking to retain moisture. |
| Styroform Cups | Reheating | Use to bring foods to a low serving temperature. Styroform will melt if foods reach a high temperature. |
| Thermometers<br>Microwave Safe, only | Cooking | Meat and candy thermometers are available |
| Wax Paper | Cooking | Use as a cover to prevent spattering and to retain moisture. |

TO TEST A CONTAINER FOR SAFE MICROWAVE OVEN USE: Fill a 1-cup glass measure with water and place it in the microwave oven along with the container to be tested; heat two minutes at **HIGH**. If the container is microwave oven safe, it should remain comfortably cool and the water should be hot. If the container is hot, it has absorbed some microwave energy and should not be used. This test cannot be used for plastic containers.

# TEMPERATURE PROBE COOKING

## EASY·MATIC TEMPERATURE

Meats, poultry or foods for slow cooking can be prepared using the Easy·Matic Temperature Probe feature. Whether you like your roast beef rare, medium or well done, the temperature probe cooks food to the degree of the doneness you prefer.

Easy·Matic Temperature offers you the convenience of eight different settings, each one having its own preprogrammed power levels and temperatures. The sensing element for the probe is located in the probe tip.

To select an Easy·Matic Temperature setting, press the TEMP control until the desired setting number is reached.

Listed below are the settings and the recommended foods for Easy·Matic Temperature.

| EASY·MATIC TEMP | |
|---|---|
| 1 | Beef (Rare) |
| 2 | Beef (Medium) |
| 3 | Beef (Well) |
| 4 | Lamb(Medium) |
| 5 | Lamb(Well) |
| 6 | Pork Roast |
| 7 | Chicken |
| 8 | Stews/Soups/Chili |

**Note:** For complete directions on how to use the temperature probe in meats and poultry, refer to the Meat and Poultry Chapters.

## PROGRAMMABLE TEMPERATURE PROBE

On some models the temperature probe can be programmed for one, two, or three power levels and temperatures ranging from 100 to 200°F. The temperature probe will sense the internal temperature of the food and will turn the oven off when the selected temperature is reached.

For **Casseroles**, Dips, and Canned Goods, insert probe into center of dish. If the dish is covered with plastic wrap, make a hole in wrap with the tip of the probe. Occasionally, it might be necessary to stir these foods. To stir, remove the probe from the food without disconnecting from the oven. Stir food and reposition probe.

For **Beverages** and Soups, insert probe into the center of the dish. For best results the probe should not be resting on the bottom of the dish.

Listed below are the recommended Powers and Temperatures for cooking casseroles, canned foods and beverages.

| ITEM | POWER | TEMP |
|---|---|---|
| Beverages(steaming)<br>with milk<br>with water or juice | <br>**MEDIUM**<br>**HIGH** | <br>160°F<br>170°F |
| Casseroles | **HIGH** | 150°F to 170°F |
| Canned Foods | **HIGH** | 160°F |
| Dips—with meat<br>with seafood<br>with cheese | **HIGH**<br>**MEDIUM**<br>**MEDIUM** | 150°F<br>150°F<br>140°F |
| Leftovers | **HIGH** | 160°F |

**Note:** For complete directions on how to use the temperature probe in meats and poultry, refer to the Meat and Poultry Chapters.

## GENERAL CARE INFORMATION FOR TEMPERATURE PROBES

Insert the Temperature probe at least one inch into the food to insure an accurate temperature reading.

Do NOT use the probe with frozen foods or a browning dish.

Clean probe with mild detergent and a soft cloth. Do NOT immerse in water or wash in the dishwasher.

Remove probe from oven cavity receptacle with a pot holder.

DO NOT USE A CONVENTIONAL MEAT THERMOMETER IN FOOD WHILE COOKING IN THE MICROWAVE OVEN. A conventional meat thermometer may be used to check the internal temperature of a food item. A microwave safe thermometer may be used during cooking.

## DEFROSTING

**PREPARING MEAT FOR FREEZING**
The finished quality of the prepared food will depend on the original quality before freezing, the care the food receives during freezing, and the techniques and times used for defrosting. Select good quality foods and freeze immediately. Proper wrapping materials should be used, and packaging techniques should be followed for best results.

**WRAPPING MATERIALS** best suited for use in the freezer are odorless, and moisture and vapor proof. Heavy-duty plastic wraps and bags, and freezer wrap are suitable. Meats may also be frozen in their store packaging for short periods of time.
Note: If aluminum foil is used for wrapping, all pieces of foil must be removed.

When **WRAPPING FOR FREEZING**, arrange meat poultry and fish and seafood in thin uniform layers. Package ground meat in 1 to 2-inch thick rectangular, square or round shapes, Chicken pieces, chops and stew meat and fish fillets will defrost more easily if frozen in 1 or 2 piece layers rather than in bulky, thick packages. To aid in separating chops, hamburger patties and fish fillets during defrosting, place two pieces of wax paper between the layers.

Remove giblet from fresh whole poultry. (The giblets may be frozen separately, if desired.) Clean and dry poultry. Tie legs and wings with string; this helps poultry keep its shape during freezing.
Remove all air before sealing plastic bags.

When using freezer paper or plastic wrap, center food to be wrapped on material. Bring two edges, up over the center and start folding down in 1-inch tucks until wrap is close to meat. Remove excess air from package. Shape ends into triangles and fold up over center. Tape securely.

LABEL package with type and cut of meat, date and weight.

FREEZE foods in a freezer which is maintained at 0°F or lower. Defrosting times given in the charts are for thoroughly frozen foods. (i.e. foods should be frozen at least 24 hours before defrosting.)

## EASY·MATIC WEIGHT DEFROST

Easy·Matic Weight Defrost can be used to defrost many cuts of meat, poultry and fish by weight.
Foods that are not recommended for Easy·Matic Weight Defrost can be defrosted using Multi·Stage Time Defrost. Follow the times and information given in the Multi·Stage Time Defrosting section.
Listed below are the recommended foods that can be defrosted on Easy·Matic Weight Defrost.

| | |
|---|---|
| **BEEF** | Roasts, Ribs, Stew Meat, Steaks, Ground Beef |
| **PORK** | Roast, Chops, Ground Pork, Frankfurters |
| **LAMB** | Roast, Chops, Ground Lamb |
| **POULTRY** | Whole or split Cornish Hens, Whole or cut up Chicken, Whole Turkey or Turkey parts |
| **FISH** | Individual Fillets, Steaks |
| **SEAFOOD** | Shrimp (medium), Sea Scallops |

**CONVERT** ounces to tenths of a pound. Meats packaged in most grocery stores are labeled with the weight in pounds and hundredths of a pound. See conversion chart.

**REMOVE WRAPPER.** Otherwise, the wrap will hold steam and juice close to the food which can cause the outer surface of the food to cook.
**PLACE ROAST FAT-SIDE DOWN** and **WHOLE POULTRY BREAST-SIDE DOWN** on a microwave roasting rack in a dish. The rack helps prevent the food from sitting in its own juice.
REMOVE ground meat from its **TRAY**. Place meat in an appropriate sized dish.

### Conversion Chart

Follow this chart to convert ounces or hundredths of a pound into tenths of a pound.

| Ounces | Hundredths of a Pound | Tenths of a Pound |
|---|---|---|
| 0 | .96–.05 | 0.0 |
| 1–2 | .06–.15 | 0.1 |
| 3–4 | .16–.25 | 0.2 |
| 5 | .26–.35 | 0.3 |
| 6–7 | .36–.45 | 0.4 |
| 8 | .46–.55 | 0.5 |
| 9–10 | .56–.65 | 0.6 |
| 11–12 | .66–.75 | 0.7 |
| 13 | .76–.85 | 0.8 |
| 14–15 | .86–.95 | 0.9 |

**Examples:** If a roast weighs 2.95 lb. or 2 lb. 14 oz., program 2.9 lb. If a roast weights 2.99 lb. or 3 lb. 0 oz., program 3.0 lb.

# DEFROSTING

To prevent overdefrosting, thin areas or edges can be shielded with strips of aluminum foil. However, when using foil, allow at least one inch of space between foil and interior oven walls. Also, if using two or more small pieces of foil to shield, place at least one inch apart from each other. This is to avoid arcing. At first or second beep, shield only when necessary. The oven beeps twice during the defrosting cycle to signal that the food needs to be turned or rearranged. Follow the directions given in the chart for the best defrosting results.

## EASY·MATIC WEIGHT DEFROSTING CHART

| CATEGORY | FIRST BEEP | SECOND BEEP | AFTER DEFROSTING |
|---|---|---|---|
| **Meat** | | | |
| Chops | Shield | Turn Over/Separate/Shield | Stand 5 min. |
| Frankfurters/Sausage | | Separate/Remove Defrosted Pieces | Stand 2 min. |
| Ground Meat | Turn Over/Remove Defrosted Pieces | Turn Over/Break Apart/Remove Defrosted Pieces | Stand 5 min. |
| Hamburger Patties | Turn Over/Separate | Turn Over/Remove Defrosted Pieces | |
| Roast | | Turn Over/Shield | Stand 30 min. in refrigerator |
| Ribs | Shield | Turn Over/Shield/Remove Defrosted Pieces | Stand 10 min. |
| Steak | | Turn Over/Shield | Stand 5 min. |
| Stew | Turn Over/Separate | Turn Over/Separate/Remove Defrosted Pieces | Stand 5 min. |
| **Poultry** | | | |
| Split Cornish Hens | | Turn Over/Shield | Stand 5 min. |
| Whole Cornish Hens | | Turn Over/Shield | Stand 10 min. Run cold water in cavity. |
| Chicken Pieces | Turn Over | Separate/Remove Defrosted Pieces | Stand 5 min. |
| Whole Chicken | | Turn Over/Shield | Stand 10 min. Run cold water in cavity. |
| Turkey Breast | | Turn Over/Shield | Stand 20 min. in refrigerator |
| **Seafood** | | | |
| Sea Scallops | Separate | Turn Over/Separate/Remove Defrosted Pieces | Stand 5 min. |
| Shrimp | Separate | Turn Over/Separate/Remove Defrosted Pieces | Stand 5 min. |
| Fish,Individual Fillets | Turn Over/Separate | Turn Over/Remove Defrosted Pieces | Run under cold water |
| Whole Fish | Turn Over | Turn Over/Shield Tail | Run under cold water |

**Note:** If necessary, shield thin ends of meat and poultry with aluminum foil.

## DEFROSTING CONTROLS

### Multi-Stage Time Defrost

All Touch Control ovens have Multi-Stage Time Defrost. To use, touch the **DEFROST** pad and program the defrosting time. The oven will divide the defrost time into eight stages: 4 defrost and 4 stand periods. During the programmed time, the oven will alternate between defrost power and stand times (no power). Follow Defrosting times and directions given in this section.

### Defrosting Fish, Seafood, Meats and Poultry

Before freezing, package meats according to directions given in ''Preparing Meat for Freezing'' on page 5.
Remove food from wrapper and set on a microwave roasting rack placed in a dish.
Set **DEFROST** and the time recommended in the chart. Turn over food two to three times during the defrost cycle. Separate chops, hamburger patties, stew meat, chicken pieces, scallops and shrimp halfway through the defrost cycle.
Remove defrosted portions from ground meat, chicken pieces, scallops and shirimp halfway through the defrost cycle. Large roasts may still be icy in center; allow to stand.
Shield thin portions with aluminum foil.
Fish and seafood should still be slightly icy.
Allow to stand to finish defrosting.
Rinse whole poultry under cold water.

## MULTI-STAGE TIME DEFROST CHART

| FOOD | MULTI-STAGE TIME DEFROST TIME (minutes per pound) | DIRECTIONS |
|---|---|---|
| **Fish and Seafood** Crabmeat | 14 to 16 | Break apart halfway through defrost time. |
| Fish Fillets | 8 to 12 | Turn over halfway through defrost time. Rinse under cold water to separate. |
| Fish Steaks | 10 to 12 | Turn over halfway through defrost time. |
| Lobster Tails | 12 to 14 | ——— |
| Sea Scallops | 16 to 20 | Break apart halfway through defrost time. Remove defrosted scallops. |
| Shrimp medium | 12 to 14 | Break apart halfway through defrost time. Remove defrosted shrimp. |
| Whole fish | 10 to 12 | Shield tail halfway through defrost time. Rinse under cold water. |
| **Beef** Ground Beef | 10 to 12 | Turn over and remove defrosted portion halfway through defrost time. |
| Liver | 12 to 14 | Drain liquid as it defrosts. Separate pieces. |

| FOOD | MULTI-STAGE TIME DEFROST TIME (minutes per pound) | DIRECTIONS |
|---|---|---|
| **Beef** Roasts | 10 to 12 | Turn over 2 to 3 times during defrost time. Shield ends. |
| Steak Sirloin | 12 to 14 | Turn over halfway through defrost time. |
| Rib or T-Bone | 8 to 10 | Turn over halfway through defrost time. |
| Flank | 8 to 10 | Turn over halfway through defrost time |
| Stew Meat | 10 to 12 | Break apart halfway through defrost time. |
| **Pork** Bacon | 6 to 8 | Defrost in original wrapper. Turn over halfway through defrost time. Center should be slightly icy. |
| Chops | 12 to 14 | Separate and turn over halfway through defrost time. |
| Ribs | 8 to 10 | Turn over halfway through defrost time. |
| Roasts | 12 to 14 | Turn over 2 to 3 times during defrost time. Shield ends. |
| **Lamb** Chops | 10 to 12 | Separate and turn over halfway through defrost time. |
| Ribs | 6 to 8 | Turn over halfway through defrost time |
| Roasts | 12 to 14 | Turn over 2 to 3 times during defrost time |
| **Poultry** Chicken Whole | 12 to 14 | Turn over 2 to 3 times during defrost time. Rinse under cold water. |
| Pieces | 8 to 10 | Separate halfway through defrost time. |
| Cutlets | 8 to 10 | Turn over halfway through defrost time. Rinse under cold water to separate. |
| Cornish Hens | 8 to 10 | Turn over halfway through defrost time. Rinse under cold water. |
| Turkey Breast | 10 to 12 | Turn over 2 to 3 times during defrost time. |

## DEFROSTING FROZEN CONVENIENCE FOODS

| ITEM | MULTI-STAGE TIME DEFROST TIME (in minutes) | DIRECTIONS |
|---|---|---|
| **Baked Goods** | | |
| Bagels | | |
| 2 | 2 to 3 | Wrap in paper towel. |
| 4 | 3 to 4 | |
| Brownies (13 oz ) | 4 to 6 | Remove from original container and place on serving plate. |
| Cheese Cake (17 oz.) | 7 to 9 | Remove from original container and place on serving plate. |
| Coffee Cake (11 to 12 oz.) | 4 to 5 | Remove from original container and place on a serving plate. |
| Cupcakes (6) (10 to 11 oz.) | 3 to 5 | Arrange in a circular pattern on oven tray. |
| Danish | | |
| 1 | 1 to 2 | |
| 2 | 3 to 4 | Place on a paper on serving plate. |
| 4 (9 oz.pkg.) | 5 to $7\frac{1}{2}$ | |
| Dinner Rolls | 3 to 5 | Wrap in paper towel. |
| Donuts | | |
| Plain or Sugar-Coated | | |
| 1 | $1\frac{1}{2}$ to 2 | Place on a paper on serving plate. |
| 2 | 2 to 3 | |
| 4 | 5 to 6 | |
| Hard Rolls (1 to $1\frac{1}{4}$ oz. ea.) | | |
| 1 | $\frac{1}{2}$ to 1 | |
| 2 | 2 to 3 | Wrap in paper towel. |
| 4 | 4 to 5 | |
| Layer Cake (17 to 18 oz.) | 3 to 5 | Remove from original container and place on a serving plate. |
| Pound Cake ($10\frac{3}{4}$ oz.) | 2 to 4 | Remove from original container and place on a serving plate. |
| **Miscellaneous** | | |
| Frozen Juice Concentrates | | Remove lid. If container is foil-lined, place in a glass measure. |
| (8 oz.) | 2 to 3 | |
| (12 oz.) | 4 to 5 | |
| Frozen Mixed Fruit (10 oz.) | 8 to 10 | Pierce pouch and place in a dish or remove metal ends and place in a dish. |
| Frozen Vegetables | | |
| (6 oz.) | 6 to 8 | Remove from box. Break apart after 3 minutes. If vegetables are in a pouch, pierce pouch. |
| (10 oz.) | 10 to 12 | |
| Non-Dairy Creamer (16 oz.) | 14 to 16 | Open carton. Shake vigorously 2 times during defrost. |
| Pancake Batter (10 oz.) | 8 to 10 | Open carton. Shake vigorously 2 times during defrost. |
| Whipped Topping (9 oz.) | 2 to 3 | Defrost in original plastic tub. |

## HEATING CANNED FOOD AND LEFTOVERS

| FOOD | COOKING TIME at HIGH (in minutes) | STAND TIME (in minutes) | DIRECTIONS |
|---|---|---|---|
| **Casseroles**<br>Individual Serving (about 1 cup)<br>Small Casseroles (about 3 cups) | 3 to 4<br>7 to 11 | 1<br>2 | Spread out for even heating. Cover with lid or plastic wrap.<br>Use $1\frac{1}{2}$-quart casserole. Stir in small amount of liquid. Cover with lid. Stir casserole 2 times during heating. |
| **Chili** (15 oz.) | 3 to $4\frac{1}{2}$ | 3 | Cover with lid. Stir once. |
| **Corned Beef Hash** ($15\frac{1}{2}$ oz.) | 3 to 4 | 3 | Cover with lid. Stir once. |
| **Gravy** ($10\frac{1}{2}$ oz.) | $2\frac{1}{2}$ to $3\frac{1}{2}$ | 1 | Stir once. |
| **Meats**<br>1 chop (about 5 oz.)<br>2 chop (about 5 oz. ea.)<br>$\frac{1}{2}$ pound meat, sliced thin<br>1 pound meat, sliced thin<br>$\frac{1}{2}$ pound meat, sliced thick<br>1 pound meat, sliced thick | 1 to $1\frac{1}{2}$<br>$2\frac{1}{2}$ to 3<br>2 to $2\frac{1}{2}$<br>$2\frac{3}{4}$ to 3<br>$2\frac{1}{2}$ to 3<br>3 to $3\frac{1}{2}$ | 1<br>1<br>1<br>1<br>1<br>1 | Arrange on plate with thick portion toward edge of dish.<br>Cover with wax paper.<br>Arrange slices flat on a plate. If desired, pour gravy over meat. Cover with wax paper. |
| **Pastries**<br>1 doughnut<br>2 doughnuts<br>4 doughnuts | $\frac{1}{4}$<br>$\frac{1}{2}$<br>$\frac{3}{4}$ to 1 | 1<br>1<br>1 | Place on paper plate. Fillings and glazes will be hotter than pastry. |
| **Pie**<br>1 slice<br>2 slices | 1 to $1\frac{1}{2}$<br>$1\frac{1}{2}$ to $2\frac{1}{2}$ | 1<br>1 | Place on a plate. |
| **Plate of Food (1)** | 3 to $3\frac{1}{2}$ | 1 | Place denser foods along edge of plate. Foods that reheat quickly, such as vegetables, should be in center of plate. Spread out mashed potatoes. Cover dish with wax paper. |
| **Pork and Beans**<br>(16 oz.)<br>($20\frac{3}{4}$ oz.) | $3\frac{1}{2}$ to $4\frac{1}{2}$<br>5 to 6 | 2<br>2 | Stir once. |
| **Rolls**<br>2<br>4 | $\frac{1}{4}$<br>$\frac{1}{2}$ to $\frac{3}{4}$ | $\frac{1}{2}$<br>1 | Wrap in a paper towel. |
| **Sandwiches**<br>Open-faced<br>1<br>2<br>Closed<br>1<br>2 | 1 to $1\frac{1}{2}$<br>$1\frac{1}{2}$ to 2<br>1 to $1\frac{1}{4}$<br>$1\frac{1}{2}$ to $1\frac{3}{4}$ | 1<br>1<br>1<br>1 | Place on a plate and cover with wax paper.<br>Wrap in a paper towel. |
| **Soup**<br>($10\frac{3}{4}$ oz. plus 1 can of water)<br>(20 oz.) | 5 to 7<br>5 to 7 | 1<br>1 | Stir after heating. |
| **Spaghetti**<br>($7\frac{3}{4}$ oz.)<br>(14 to 19 oz.) | $2\frac{1}{2}$ to $3\frac{1}{2}$<br>$4\frac{1}{2}$ to $5\frac{1}{2}$ | 1<br>1 | Stir once. |
| **Vegetables**<br>(8 oz.)<br>(16 to 17 oz.) | 2 to 3<br>3 to 4 | 1<br>1 | Stir once. |

## FROZEN CONVENIENCE FOODS

Most frozen convenience foods have microwave heating directions on the back of the package. Refer to these directions for recommended power levels, heating times and general instructions.

General Directions for Heating Frozen Convenience Foods.

**Arrange small items**, such as appetizers, in a **circular pattern** on a paper towel lined plate.

**Arrange fried chicken** or **fried fish** between 2 pieces of paper towels on a plate. Coating will not be crisp after heating.

**Pierce pouch** vegetables or entrees with a fork or knife. Place pouch in a dish before heating.

Frozen foods packaged in **microwave-safe containers** should be heated according to manufacturer's directions.

Frozen Foods in **metal containers deeper than 3/4 inch**, such as lasagna or baked stuffed potatoes, must be removed from the foil container and placed in an appropriately sized microwave-safe container. Heat covered with lid or plastic wrap. Note: if food is difficult to remove from container, rinse bottom of container with hot water.

Frozen foods in **metal containers less than 3/4 inch**, may be heated in the container in the microwave oven.

**To heat frozen dinners in foil containers,** remove dinner from box.
If there is a foil cover, remove it. Some foods, such as bread, french fries or batter type desserts such as brownies, do not microwave well. Remove these types of food from tray.
Cover tray except desserts with plastic wrap.
Heat according to manufacturers' directions.
Place foil tray in center of oven.
Foil tray should not touch oven walls or other metal. Heat only 1 foil tray in the oven at a time.

## CONVERTING FAVORITE RECIPES

Select recipes that convert easily to microwave cooking such as casseroles, stews, baked chicken, fish and vegetable dishes. The results from foods such as broiled meats, cooked souffles or two-crust pies would be less than satisfactory. Never attempt to deep fat fry in your microwave oven. A basic rule, when converting conventional recipes to microwave recipes, is to cut the suggested cooking time by one-fourth. Also, find a similar microwave recipe and adapt that time and power setting. Season meats with herbs and spices before cooking; salt after cooking. Stew meats are not browned before cooking. Omit any oil or fat that would be used for browning. Cut stew meat into 1 1/2-inch pieces. Cut carrots, potatoes and other firm vegetables into small pieces. Carrots should be thinly sliced and potatoes cut into sixteenths. Reduce liquid by one-fourth. Cover with lid and cook at HIGH to bring liquid to a boil and cook at LOW until tender. Stir occasionally. Casseroles microwave well. Cut foods into uniform pieces. Condensed soup makes a good base for casseroles. Select a dish that is large enough to allow for stirring. Cooking with a lid or plastic wrap reduces cooking time. Stir occasionally during cooking. To keep crumb toppings crisp, sprinkle on before stand time.

## APPETIZER PÂTÉ

**1 pound chicken livers, halved**
**1/2 cup chicken broth**
**1 medium onion, chopped**
**1/4 teaspoon thyme**
**4 slices bacon, cooked and crumbled (see page 23)**
**1/4 cup butter or margarine, softened**
**1 tablespoon sherry, optional**
**1/2 teaspoon garlic salt**
**Dash pepper**
**Parsley flakes**

**Yield:** 1 1/3 Cups

In 1 1/2 quart bowl, combine livers, broth, onion and thyme. Cover with plastic wrap. Cook at **HIGH** 3 to 5 minutes and at **MEDIUM** 3 to 4 minutes, or until livers are tender; stir once. Drain and reserve 1/4 cup liquid. In electric blender or food processor, puree liver and onion mixture, reserved liquid, bacon, butter, sherry, garlic and pepper until smooth. Spoon into crock or small bowl; sprinkle with parsley and chill. Serve as a spread with crackers.

## COCKTAIL MEATBALLS

**1/2 pound ground beef**
**1 egg, beaten**
**1/4 cup Italian flavored dry bread crumbs**
**1 clove garlic, finely chopped**
**2 tablespoons finely chopped green onion**
**1/2 teaspoon salt**
**1/4 teaspoon basil leaves, crushed**
**Dash pepper**
**1/2 cup grape jelly**
**1/2 cup chili sauce**
**1 tablespoon prepared mustard**

**Yield:** 24 Meatballs

In medium bowl, combine meat, egg, bread crumbs, garlic, onion and seasonings. Mix lightly. Shape into 24 bite-size meatballs. In 2-quart casserole, combine jelly, chili sauce and mustard. Mix until well blended. Add meatballs. Cover with lid. Cook at **HIGH** 6 1/2 minutes and at **MEDIUM-LOW** 9 to 10 minutes. Stir twice. Let stand, uncovered, 3 minutes before serving.

## STUFFED MUSHROOMS

**1 pound medium mushrooms (about 24), cleaned**
**4 slices bacon, chopped**
**1 small onion, finely chopped**
**1/2 cup dry bread crumbs**
**1/3 cup white wine or water**
**1/4 cup greated Parmesan cheese**
**1/8 teaspoon pepper**

**Yield:** 24 Mushrooms

Remove stems from mushrooms. Finely chop enough stems to equal 1 cup; set aside.
Place bacon and onion in bowl. Cook at **HIGH** 5 to 6 1/2 minutes, or until bacon is crisp and onion is tender; stir once. Drain. Stir in chopped mushroom stems, bread crumbs, wine, cheese and pepper.
Stuff mushroom caps with bread crumb mixture. Arrange half of mushrooms in a circular pattern in a 9-inch pie plate. Cook at **HIGH** 4 1/2 to 6 1/2 minutes. Let stand, uncovered, 2 minutes before serving. Repeat procedure with remaining mushrooms.
***Variation: For SPINACH Stuffed Mushrooms,*** partially defrost 1 package (12 oz.) frozen spinach souffle. Cut into squares and place in mushroom caps; sprinkle, if desired, with onion salt. Heat as directed above.

## CHEESE AND SPINACH CRUSTLESS QUICHE

**4 eggs**
**1/3 cup half'n half**
**1 1/2 cups (6 oz.) shredded Swiss cheese**
**1 package (10 oz.) frozen chopped spinach, cooked and drained (see page 9)**
**4 slices bacon, crisp-cooked and crumbled (see page 23)**
**1 teaspoon lemon juice**
**1/2 teaspoon salt**

**Yield:** 10 Servings

Beat eggs with half'n half until light and fluffy in medium bowl. Blend in cheese, spinach, bacon, lemon juice and salt. Pour into lightly greased 9-inch quiche dish. Cover with wax paper. Cook at **MEDIUM** 10 to 12 minutes. Quiche is done when knife inserted near center comes out clean. Let stand, uncovered, 10 minutes. Cut into 10 pieces to serve.

## HOLIDAY CHEESE BALL

**2 packages (3 oz ea.) cream cheese, cubed**
**3 cups (12 oz.) shredded Cheddar cheese**
**3 tablespoons sherry**
**1/4 teaspoon onion powder**
**1/8 teaspoon garlic powder**
**1/8 teaspoon Worcestershire sauce**
**1/2 cup finely chopped nuts**

**Yield:** 1 Ball

In medium bowl, combine cheeses, wine, onion, garlic and Worcestershire. Cook at **MEDIUM** 4 1/2 to 5 minutes, or until cheese is melted, stir once. With electric mixer, beat until smooth. Chill 1 to 2 hours, or until semi-firm. Shape into ball and roll in nuts, serve with crackers. Refrigerate leftovers.
To reheat, cook at **LOW** 2 to 3 1/2 minutes, or until spreadable.

## LAREDO-STYLE NACHOS

**20 corn, taco or tortilla chips**
**1 can (10 oz.) bean dip**
**Guacamole, optional**
**Jalapeño peppers, sliced, optional**
**Shredded Monterey Jack cheese**

**Yield:** 20 Hors d'oeuvres

Spread 20 chips with bean dip and guacamole; top with peppers and cheese. Arrange on serving plate. Cook at **HIGH** 1 to 2 minutes, or until cheese is melted. Serve immediately. Repeat procedure as desired.

## NUTS AND BOLTS PARTY MIX

**1/2 cup butter or margarine**
**2 tablespoons Worcestershire sauce**
**1/2 teaspoon garlic power**
**2 cups bite-size corn squares cereal**
**2 cups bite-size rice squares cereal**
**2 cups bite-size wheat squares cereal**
**1 cup salted peanuts**
**1 cup thin pretzel sticks**

**Yield:** 2 Quarts

Place butter in 4-quart casserole. Cook at **MEDIUM-LOW** 2 to 2 1/2 minutes, or until butter is melted. Stir in Worcestershire and garlic powder. Add remaining ingredients, stir well. Cook at **HIGH** 6 to 8 minutes, or until butter is absorbed and mixture is crisp; stir occasionally. Cool before serving or storing.

## SPICED WALNUTS

**1 pound shelled walnut halves**
**3 tablespoons butter or margarine, cut into 6 pieces**
**1/4 cup sugar**
**2 teaspoons cinnamon**
**1/4 teaspoon nutmeg**
**1/4 teaspoon cloves**

**Yield:** 1 Pound

Place walnuts in 3-quart casserole. Cook at **HIGH** 9 to 10 minutes; stir twice.
Meanwhile, combine sugar, cinnamon, nutmeg and cloves; stir until blended.
Stir butter into hot nuts; mix until butter is melted and nuts are lightly coated. If necessary to melt butter, cook at **HIGH** 10 to 20 seconds. Add sugar and spice mixture to nuts. Stir well until evenly coated. Allow to cool. Store in covered container.

## HORSERADISH CHEESE VEGETABLE DIP

**1 package (8 oz.) cream cheese, cubed**
**1 1/2 cups (6 oz.) shredded Cheddar cheese**
**1/2 cup milk**
**2 tablespoons thinly sliced green onions**
**1 tablespoon Worcestershire sauce**
**1 tablespoon horseradish**
**1/2 teaspoon hot-pepper sauce**

**Yield:** 3 Cups

Place cream cheese and Cheddar cheese in 1 1/2-quart casserole. Heat at **MEDIUM** 3 1/2 minutes, or until melted, stir once. Add milk, sliced green onions, Worcestershire sauce, horseradish and hot-pepper sauce. Cook at **HIGH** 2 1/2 to 3 minutes. Stir with whisk until well blended. Serve with bite-size pieces of raw vegetables, such as broccoli, cauliflower, celery, cucumbers or cherry tomatoes.

## CHILI CON QUESO

**1 can (16 oz.) refried beans**
**1 can (10 oz.) enchilada sauce**
**2 cups (8 oz.) shredded Monterey Jack or Cheddar cheese**
**1/4 cup chopped green onions**
**1 teaspoon hot-pepper sauce**
**Tortilla chips**

**Yield:** 4 Cups

In 2 quart casserole, combine beans, sauce, cheese, green onions and hot-pepper sauce; stir well. Cook at **HIGH** 8 to 9 minutes, or until cheese is melted; stir twice. Serve warm with Tortilla Chips.

## PEANUT BRITTLE

**1 cup sugar**
**1/2 cup light corn syrup**
**1 cup salted peanuts**
**1 teaspoon butter or margarine**
**1 teaspoon vanilla**
**1 teaspoon baking soda**

**Yield:** 1 1/2 Pounds

In 2-quart glass-ceramic casserole, combine sugar and corn syrup; stir. Cook at **HIGH** 4 minutes. Add peanuts; stir well. Cook at **HIGH** for an additional 3 1/2 minutes; add butter and vanilla, stirring well. Cook at **HIGH** 1 1/2 minutes. Add baking soda; stir gently until light and foamy. Immediately pour mixture onto buttered cookie sheet. Spread thinly. Cool; break into small pieces.

## BUTTERSCOTCH FUDGE

**3 cups sugar**
**3/4 cup butter or margarine**
**1 can (5 1/3 oz.) evaporated milk**
**1 package (12 oz.) butterscotch flavored pieces***
**1 jar (7 1/2 oz.) marshmallow creme**
**1 cup chopped walnuts**
**1 teaspoon vanilla**

**Yield:** 3 Pounds

In 2 1/2-quart casserole, combine sugar, butter and milk. Cook at **HIGH** 8 to 10 minutes, or until sugar is dissolved; stir twice. Add remaining ingredients and stir until butterscotch is melted. Turn into well greased 11x7-inch dish. Cool; cut into squares to serve.

****Variation: For CHOCOLATE Fudge,*** *use 1 package (12 oz.) semisweet chocolate pieces.*

## RAISIN CLUSTERS

**8 squares (1 oz. ea.) semi-sweet chocolate**
**2/3 cup sweetened condensed milk**
**1 cup raisins***

**Yield:** 2 Dozen

In medium glass bowl, heat chocolate at **MEDIUM-LOW** 3 to 4 minutes, or until chocolate is melted; stir in milk until smooth, then raisins. Drop by teaspoonfuls onto greased wax paper lined cookie sheet; chill.

****Variations:***
***For ELEPHANT Clusters,*** *use 1 cup unsalted peanuts for raisins.*
***For CHINESE Clusters,*** *use 1 cup crisp chow mein noodles for raisins.*

## JAM BARS

**1/4 cup butter or margarine, softened (see page 48)**
**1/4 cup sugar**
**1 egg**
**1/2 cup flour**
**1/4 cup ground walnuts**
**1/2 teaspoon grated lemon peel**
**1/4 teaspoon cinnamon**
**1/8 teaspoon salt**
**1/2 cup raspberry or strawberry jam**

**Topping:**
**1/2 cup flour**
**1/4 cup packed brown sugar**
**3 tablespoons butter or margarine, softened (see page 48)**

**Yield:** 16 Bars

Cream butter and sugar with electric mixer. Add egg, flour, walnuts, lemon peel, cinnamon and salt. Mix well. Pat mixture into 8-inch square dish. Cook at **HIGH** 2 1/2 to 3 1/2 minutes, or until center is slightly firm.
Meanwhile, mix together topping ingredients until mixture resembles coarse crumbs. Spread jam on top of baked crust; sprinkle topping over jam. Cook at **HIGH** 3 to 3 1/2 minutes, or until jam bubbles around edge. Let stand until cool.

## S'MORES

**8 graham cracker squares**
**2 milk chocolate candy bars (1 1/4 oz. ea.), halved**
**4 marshmallows**

**Yield:** 4 Cookies

Arrange 4 graham crackers in circle on paper plate. Top with chocolate and marshmallow. Heat at **HIGH** 30 to 40 seconds. Top with remaining crackers. Let stand 2 minutes.

## SCRAMBLED EGGS

Beat eggs and 1 tablespoon milk and dash salt for each egg. Pour into greased glass container. Cook at **MEDIUM** according to time in the chart. Stir two-thirds of the way through the cooking time. Stir and let stand. Eggs will continue to cook during stand time and should be slightly undercooked after cooking.

| Eggs | Container | Cooking Time (in minutes) | Stand Time (in minutes) |
|---|---|---|---|
| 1 | 1 cup glass measure | 3/4 to 1 1/4 | 1 |
| 2 | 1 cup glass measure | 1 1/2 to 2 | 1 1/2 |
| 4 | 1 quart bowl | 3 1/4 to 3 3/4 | 1 1/2 |
| 6 | 1 1/2 quart bowl | 4 3/4 to 5 1/2 | 2 |

## POACHED EGGS

Place 1 1/2 cups hot water in 2 quart casserole and heat at **HIGH** 5 to 7 minutes, or until water boils. Break egg(s) into boiling water and with toothpick pierce egg yolk twice and egg white several times. Cook at **MEDIUM** according to the time given in the chart. Let stand.

| Eggs | Cooking Time (in minutes) | Stand Time (in minutes) |
|---|---|---|
| 1 | 1/2 to 3/4 | 1 |
| 2 | 1 to 1 1/4 | 2 |
| 4 | 1 3/4 to 2 | 2 |

## EGGS BENEDICT

**1 package (1 1/4 oz.) hollandaise sauce mix**
**Ingredients as sauce mix package directs**
**4 eggs**
**4 thin slices cooked ham**
**2 English muffins, split and toasted**

**Yield:** 4 Servings

Combine sauce mix and ingredients as package directs in 2-cup glass measure. Cook at **HIGH** 2 to 3 minutes, or until sauce is thickened; stir once. Prepare Poached Eggs according to chart above. While eggs are standing, cook ham. Arrange ham in single layer on paper towel-lined paper plate. Cook at **MEDIUM** 1 to 1 1/2 minutes. To serve, place ham on muffin; top with egg, then sauce. If necessary, reheat at **MEDIUM** 1/2 to 1 minute.

## BASIC OMELET

**1 tablespoon butter or margarine**
**2 eggs**
**2 tablespoons milk**
**1/8 teaspoon salt**
**Dash pepper**

**Yield:** 1 Serving

Cook butter in 9-inch glass pie plate at **LOW** 2 minutes.
Turn plate to coat bottom with butter. Meanwhile, combine remaining ingredients; pour into pie plate. Cover with plastic wrap. Cook at **MEDIUM** 2 to 3 1/2 minutes, or until omelet is almost set; stir after 1 minute. Let stand, covered, 2 minutes. With spatula, loosen edges of omelet from plate; fold into thirds to serve.

***Variations:***
***For CHEESE Omelet,*** *before folding, sprinkle 1/4 cup shredded cheese down center of omelet.*

***For HAM Omelet,*** *before folding, sprinkle 1/4 cup finely chopped cooked ham down center of omelet.*

***For HERB Omelet,*** *blend 1/8 teaspoon basil, thyme or crushed rosemary with eggs and milk.*

***For JELLY Omelet,*** *before folding, spoon 1/4 cup jelly down center of omelet.*

## BAKED EGGS IN BOLOGNA CUPS

**4 slices bologna**
**4 eggs**
**Salt and pepper to taste**

**Yield:** 4 Servings

For each serving, line each custard cup (6 oz. ea.) with bologna. Break egg into center. With toothpick, pierce egg yolk twice and egg white several times. Season with salt and pepper. Cover each cup with plastic wrap. Cook at **MEDIUM** 2 to 3 minutes. Let stand, covered, 2 minutes before serving.

***Note: For TWO baked eggs,*** *follow above procedure; halve all ingredients. Cook 1 1/4 to 1 3/4 minutes. Let stand 1 minute.*

*Eggs should not be hard-cooked in their shells in a microwave oven. Pressure will build up and the egg will explode.*

## CAULIFLOWER AND CARROT QUICHE

**1 1/2 cups coarsely chopped cauliflower**
**1 carrot, shredded**
**1 tablespoon water**
**1 9-inch pie shell, baked (see page 32)**
**1 cup (4 oz.) shredded Swiss cheese**
**1/4 cup grated Parmesan cheese**
**3 eggs**
**1 cup (1/2 pt.) heavy cream**
**1/8 teaspoon pepper**

**Yield:** 10 Servings

In 1-quart bowl, combine cauliflower, carrot and water. Cover with plastic wrap. Cook at **HIGH** 5 to 7 minutes. Stir once. Sprinkle vegetables into pie shell. Sprinkle cheese over vegetables.
Pour cream into 2-cup measure. Cook at **MEDIUM** 2 to 2 1/4 minutes.
Meanwhile, beat eggs in small bowl. Stir a little hot cream into eggs. Blend eggs back into cream. Add pepper. Pour mixture over ingredients in pie shell. Cook at **MEDIUM-LOW** 13 to 15 minutes. Let stand 10 minutes.

## MACARONI AND CHEESE

**1 package (8 oz.) elbow macaroni, cooked and drained (see page 30)**
**3/4 pound pasteurized process cheese spread, cut into cubes**
**3/4 to 1 cup milk**
**1/2 to 3/4 teaspoon salt**
**1/4 teaspoon pepper**
**1/8 teaspoon dry mustard, optional**
**Buttered bread, crumbs**

**Yield:** 4 Servings

In 3-quart casserole, combine macaroni, cheese, milk, salt, pepper and mustard. Cover with lid. Cook at **MEDIUM** 9 to 10 minutes; stir twice. Top with bread crumbs and cook, uncovered, at **MEDIUM** 3 minutes. Let stand, covered, 10 minutes before serving.

***Variation:*** *Use 1/2 cup tomato sauce for 1/4 cup milk and 1/8 teaspoon oregano for dry mustard.*

## SIMPLE LASAGNA

**1/2 pound ground beef**
**1 jar (15 1/2 oz.) spaghetti sauce**
**1 can (8 oz.) tomato sauce**
**1 teaspoon oregano**
**1/2 teaspoon garlic powder**
**1 container (15 to 16 oz.) ricotta or cottage cheese (about 1 1/2 cups)**
**1/4 cup grated Parmesan cheese**
**1 egg, slightly beaten**
**1/4 teaspoon salt**
**1/8 teaspoon pepper**
**2 cups (8 oz.) shredded mozzarella cheese, divided 8 lasagna noodles, cooked and drained**

**Yield:** 6 Servings

Crumble ground beef in large bowl. Cook at **HIGH** 3 to 4 minutes, or until beef is browned; stir once. Drain. Stir in spaghetti sauce, tomato sauce, oregano and garlic powder.
Meanwhile, combine ricotta cheese, Parmesan cheese, egg, salt, pepper and 1 cup mozzarella cheese. Spoon half of sauce into 13x9-inch dish. Top with 4 noodles and cheese mixture. Top with remaining noodles and sauce.
Cover with plastic wrap. Cook at **HIGH** 10 minutes and at **MEDIUM-LOW** 15 to 20 minutes, or until noodles are tender. If necessary, shield ends of dish with foil during last 10 minutes of cooking.
Sprinkle with remaining mozzarella cheese.
Let stand, tented with foil, 15 minutes before serving.

## MINI-PIZZA SNACKS

**2 English muffins, split and toasted**
**1/4 to 1/2 cup spaghetti sauce**
**1/4 cup (1 oz.) shredded mozzarella cheese**
**Oregano**

**Yield:** 2 Servings

Arrange muffins on paper plate. Spread with spaghetti sauce. Top with cheese and season with oregano. Cook at **MEDIUM** 1 to 2 minutes, or until cheese is melted.

***Note: For ONE Serving,*** *follow above procedure; halve all ingredients. Cook 1/2 to 1 minute.*

## DIRECTIONS FOR PREPARING/COOKING FISH AND SEAFOOD

**Use fresh** or **defrosted**, cleaned fish.

**Arrange fish** in a single layer in dish. For best results, avoid overlapping edges, as this will prevent fish from cooking evenly.

**Place thicker sections** toward edge of the dish (i.e. tail sections toward center).

**Arrange shrimp** and **scallops** in a single layer in dish.

**Cook fish** or **seafood** covered with plastic wrap.

**Rearrange** or stir shrimp or scallops halfway through cooking.

**Cook** according to directions given in chart.

**Test for doneness** before adding extra cooking time.
The color of seafood and fish should be opaque and the fish should flake easily when tested with a fork. If undercooked, return to oven and cook 15 to 30 seconds longer at recommended power level.

**Let stand**, covered, 3 to 5 minutes before serving.
Stand time allows the internal temperature to equalize throughout the food and thereby finishes the cooking process.

## FISH AND SEAFOOD CHART

| FISH OR SEAFOOD | AMOUNT | POWER | APPROX. COOKING TIME (in minutes) |
|---|---|---|---|
| **Fish Fillets** | 1 lb. | **HIGH** | 4 1/2 to 6 |
| **Fish Steaks**, (1-inch thick) | 1 lb. | **HIGH** | 5 to 6 |
| **Sea Scallops** | 1 lb. | **MEDIUM** | 7 1/2 to 8 |
| **Shrimp** medium size (shelled and cleaned) | 1 lb. | **MEDIUM** | 4 1/2 to 6 |
| **Whole fish** (stuffed or unstuffed) | 1 to 1 1/2 lb. | **HIGH** | 6 to 7 |

## FILLET PROVENCALE

**1 medium onion, sliced**
**2 tablespoons butter or margarine**
**1 clove garlic, finely chopped**
**1 can (16 oz.) stewed tomatoes, chopped**
**1 jar (4 1/2oz.) sliced mushrooms, drained**
**1/4 cup white wine**
**1/4 teaspoon basil**
**6 flounder fillets (about 1/4 lb. ea.)**
**Salt**

**Yield:** 6 Servings

In 8-inch square dish, combine onion, butter and garlic. Cover with plastic wrap. Cook at **HIGH** 4 minutes. Stir in tomatoes, mushrooms, wine and basil. Cover. Cook at **HIGH** 4 minutes and at **MEDIUM** 3 to 5 minutes. Meanwhile, season fish with salt, skin-side only. Roll-up (skin-side in) and arrange seam-side down in sauce by edge of dish. Spoon sauce over fish. Cook, covered, at **HIGH** 5 to 7 minutes, or until fish flakes when tested with a fork. Let stand, covered, 5 minutes.

## FILLET AMANDINE

**3 tablespoons butter or margarine**
**3 tablespoons slivered almonds**
**1/2 pound fish fillets**
**Salt and pepper to taste**
**Lemon juice**
**Parsley flakes**

**Yield:** 2 Servings

Place butter and almonds in 8-inch square dish. Cook at **HIGH** 3 to 4 minutes; stir once. Dip fillets in butter and arrange in same dish; spoon almonds and butter on top of fish. Season with salt and pepper. Sprinkle with lemon juice. Cover with plastic wrap. Cook at **HIGH** 4 to 5 minutes, or until fish flakes when tested with a fork.
Let stand, covered, 3 minutes; sprinkle with parsley before serving.

## TARRAGON HALIBUT STEAKS

**3 tablespoons lemon juice**
**2 tablespoons oil**
**1 teaspoon salt**
**1/2 teaspoon paprika**
**1/2 teaspoon onion powder**
**1/2 teaspoon tarragon**
**4 halibut steaks, 1-inch thick (about 8 oz. ea.)**

**Yield:** 4 Servings

In small bowl, mix lemon juice, oil, salt, paprika, onion powder and tarragon until blended. Arrange halibut steaks in 8-inch square dish. Pour marinade over steaks. Cover and marinate 1 hour. Cook at **HIGH** 8 to 11 minutes, or until fish flakes easily, Let stand, covered, 3 to 5 minutes before serving.

## FLOUNDER WITH SHRIMP SAUCE

**4 flounder fillets (about 1/4 lb. ea.)**
**1 can (10 3/4 oz.) condensed cream of shrimp soup**
**1/4 cup white wine or milk**
**1/2 cup (2 oz.) shredded Swiss cheese**
**Parsley or slivered almonds**

**Yield:** 4 Servings

Roll up fillets and arrange seam-side down in 8-inch square dish. Combine soup, wine and cheese; spoon over fillets. Cover with plastic wrap. Cook at **MEDIUM** 11 to 12 minutes, or until fish is done. Let stand, covered, 5 minutes. Sprinkle with parsley or almonds before serving.

## OPEN-FACED TUNA TEMPTER

**1 can (7 oz.) tuna, drained and flaked**
**1/3 cup mayonnaise**
**Celery seed**
**Onion powder**
**Salt and pepper**
**4 slices whole wheat bread, toasted**
**4 thin slices tomato**
**4 slices American cheese**

**Yield:** 4 servings

Combine tuna and mayonnaise; season with celery, onion, salt and pepper. Spread tuna on toast; top with tomato. On paper plate, cook 2 sandwiches at **MEDIUM** 1 to 1 1/2 minutes; top with cheese. Cook at **MEDIUM** 1 minute, or until cheese is melted. Repeat procedure with remaining sandwiches.

## SWEET AND SOUR FILLETS

**1 pound flounder fillets**
**1/4 cup packed brown sugar**
**1 tablespoon cornstarch**
**1 can (8 oz.) pineapple chunks, drained; reserve syrup**
**1/2 medium green pepper, cut into thin strips**
**1/4 cup cider vinegar**
**1 tablespoon soy sauce**
**2 green onions, thinly sliced**
**1/8 teaspoon garlic powder**
**1/4 cup slivered almonds, toasted (see page 48)**

**Yield:** 4 Servings

In 8-inch square dish, arrange fillets in single layer. Cover with plastic wrap. Cook at **HIGH** 5 to 7 minutes, or until fish flakes easily with fork. Let stand, covered, 5 minutes.
Meanwhile, in 1-quart casserole, combine sugar and cornstarch. Stir in reserved pineapple syrup. Add green pepper, vinegar, soy sauce, green onions and garlic powder. Cook at **HIGH** 3 to 4 minutes, or until mixture is thickened; stir twice. Stir in pineapple chunks. Arrange fillets on serving dish. Spoon mixture over fillets.

## FISHERMAN'S POT

**1 large onion, thinly sliced**
**1 stalk celery, thinly sliced**
**1 clove garlic, finely chopped**
**1 can (28 oz.) whole tomatoes, chopped**
**1 cup chicken broth***
**2 tablespoons finely chopped parsley**
**1 teaspoon salt**
**1/8 teaspoon thyme leaves**
**1 pound fish fillets, cut into chunks**
**1/4 cup white wine**

**Yield:** 4 Servings

In 3-quart casserole, combine onion, celery and garlic. Cover with lid. Cook at **HIGH** 6 to 7 minutes; stir once. Add tomatoes, broth, parsley, salt and thyme. Cook, covered, at **HIGH** 8 minutes and at **MEDIUM** 9 to 10 minutes; stir once. Add fish and wine. Cook, covered, at **MEDIUM** 4 to 7 minutes, or until fish is tender, stir once. Let stand, covered, 5 minutes before serving.

****Substitution:** Use 1 bottle (8 oz.) clam juice for chicken broth.*

## SHRIMP SCAMPI

**1 clove garlic, finely chopped**
**1/3 cup butter or margarine**
**1/4 cup chopped parsley**
**1/2 teaspoon salt**
**1 1/4 pounds medium shrimp, shelled and cleaned**
**1 tablespoon lemon juice**

**Yield:** 4 Servings.

Combine garlic and butter in 1-quart casserole. Cook at **HIGH** 1 1/2 to 2 minutes. Add parsley and salt. Stir in shrimp, coating each with butter sauce. Cover with plastic wrap. Cook at **MEDIUM** 5 to 6 minutes, stir once. Let stand, covered, 3 minutes. Sprinkle lemon juice over shrimp before serving.

## SCALLOPS IN WHITE WINE

**1/4 cup butter or margarine**
**1 medium onion, chopped**
**2 cloves garlic, finely chopped**
**1 pound sea scallops**
**1/4 cup dry white wine**
**1/2 teaspoon salt**
**1/4 teaspoon thyme**
**1/8 teaspoon pepper**
**1/2 cup chopped parsley**
**1 tablespoon lemon juice**

**Yield:** 4 Servings

Combine butter, onion and garlic in 2-quart casserole. Cover with lid. Cook at **HIGH** 2 to 3 minutes, or until onion is tender. Stir in scallops, wine, salt, thyme and pepper; cover. Cook at **MEDIUM** 6 to 8 minutes; stir once. Stir in parsley and lemon juice. If desired, serve with rice.

## SIMPLE SEAFOOD NEWBURG

**1 can (10 3/4 oz.) condensed cream of mushroom soup**
**1 package (10 oz.) frozen peas, defrosted (see page 9)**
**1/4 cup milk or half'n half**
**1 pound seafood, cooked (see page 17) and cut into bite-size pieces**
**1 jar (2 1/2 oz.) sliced mushrooms, drained**
**2 to 3 tablespoons sherry**

**Yield:** 4 Servings

In 1 1/2-quart casserole, combine soup, peas and milk. Cover with lid. Cook at **MEDIUM** 4 to 5 minutes; stir once. Add remaining ingredients. Cook, covered, at **MEDIUM** 4 to 6 minutes, or until heated through; stir once. Let stand, covered, 3 minutes before serving.

## SHRIMP ORIENTAL

**1/2 cup water**
**3 tablespoons soy sauce**
**2 tablespoons sherry**
**1 envelope chicken bouillon**
**1/4 teaspoon crushed red pepper**
**1/4 teaspoon ginger**
**1 clove garlic, finely chopped**
**1 tablespoon cornstarch**
**1 package (6 oz.) frozen pea pods, defrosted and drained (see page 9)**
**1 can (8 oz.) bamboo shoots, drained**
**1 1/4 pounds large shrimp, shelled and cleaned**
**4 green onions, sliced**
**Hot cooked rice, optional**

**Yield:** 4 Servings

In 3-quart casserole, combine water, soy sauce, sherry, bouillon, red pepper, ginger and garlic. Blend in cornstarch until smooth. Cover with lid. Cook at **HIGH** 3 1/2 to 4 minutes. Add pea pods, bamboo shoots, shrimp and green onions; stir to coat. Cover with lid. Cook at **MEDIUM** 6 to 8 minutes, or until shrimp are opaque; stir once. Let stand, covered, 5 minutes before serving. If desired, serve over rice.

## BUSY DAY TUNA CASSEROLE

**1 can (6 1/2 oz.) tuna, drained and flaked**
**4 cups (8 oz.) noodles, cooked and drained (see page 30)**
**1 can (10 3/4 oz.) condensed cream of celery soup**
**1 can (4 oz.) sliced mushrooms, drained**
**1 package (10 oz.) frozen peas, defrosted (see page 9)**
**3/4 cup milk**
**2 tablespoons chopped pimento**
**1 cup crushed potato chips**

**Yield:** 4—6 Servings

In 3-quart casserole, combine tuna, noodles, soup, mushrooms, peas, milk and pimento; mix well. Cover with wax paper. Cook at **HIGH** 6 minutes and at **MEDIUM-LOW** 10 to 12 minutes. Stir twice.
Top with potato chips; let stand, uncovered, 3 minutes.

## BAKED APPLES

**4 large baking apples (about 8 to 10 oz. ea.)**
**1/4 cup packed brown sugar**
**2 tablespoons finely chopped nuts or raisins**
**1/4 teaspoon cinnamon**
**2 tablespoons butter or margarine**
**1/4 cup water**

**Yield:** 4 Servings

Core apples, leaving small plug in blossom end; peel skin 1-inch from top. Combine sugar, nuts and cinnamon; fill apples with mixture.
Arrange apples in 8-inch square dish. Dot with butter and sprinkle with water. Cover with plastic wrap. Cook at **HIGH** 11 to 13 minutes. Let stand, 5 minutes; serve warm or chilled, spooning sauce over apples.

***Note:For TWO Servings,*** *follow above procedure. Halve all ingredients; cook apples 5 to 7 minutes.*

***For ONE Serving,*** *cook apples 2 1/2 to 3 1/2 minutes.*

## PEACH BETTY

**2 cans (16 oz. ea.) sliced peaches, drained**
**1 tablespoon flour**
**1/4 teaspoon cinnamon**

**Topping:**
**1/2 cup packed brown sugar**
**1/4 cup plain dry bread crumbs**
**1 teaspoon cinnamon**
**1/2 teaspoon nutmeg**
**1/4 cup butter or margarine**
**2/3 cup quick cooking oats**
**1/2 cup chopped walnuts**

**Yield:** 6 Servings

In 1 1/2-quart casserole, combine peaches, flour and 1/4 teaspoon cinnamon. In medium bowl, combine brown sugar, bread crumbs, 1 teaspoon cinnamon and nutmeg. Cut in butter until mixture resembles coarse crumbs. Stir in oats and nuts. Sprinkle over peaches. Cover with lid. Cook at **MEDIUM** 16 to 18 minutes, or until hot and bubbly. Let stand, uncovered, 20 minutes.

## CHUNKY APPLESAUCE

**3 pounds baking apples, peeled, cored and sliced (about 5 1/2 cups)**
**3/4 cup sugar or to taste**
**1/2 cup water**
**1/2 to 1 teaspoon cinnamon**

**Yield:** 5 1/2 Cups

Combine all ingredients in large glass bowl. Cover with wax paper. Cook at **HIGH** 9 to 11 minutes, or until apples are tender; stir once. Let stand, covered, 7 minutes. Mash apples until chunky; serve warm or chilled.

## BAKED GRAPEFRUIT

**2 medium grapefruits**
**8 teaspoons packed brown sugar, granulated sugar or maple syrup**
**Cinnamon**

**Yield:** 4 Servings

With sharp knife, cut each grapefruit in half; remove seeds and cut around each section. Arrange grapefruit on glass oven tray. Sprinkle with brown sugar. Cook at **HIGH** 5 to 6 minutes. Sprinkle with cinnamon before serving.

***Note: For TWO Servings,*** *follow above procedure. Halve all ingredients, cook 2 to 3 minutes*
***For ONE Serving,*** *cook 1 to 2 minutes.*

## BANANAS FOSTER

**1/3 cup packed brown sugar**
**1/4 cup butter or margarine**
**1 tablespoon water**
**1 teaspoon lemon juice**
**1 teaspoon rum extract**
**1/4 teaspoon nutmeg**
**3 bananas, diagonally sliced 1/2-inch thick**
**1/2 cup heavy cream, whipped**
**1/3 cup coconut, toasted, (see page 48)**

**Yield:** 4 Servings

In 1 1/2-quart glass bowl, combine brown sugar, butter, water, lemon juice, rum extract, and nutmeg. Cook at **HIGH** 3 1/2 to 4 minutes; stir twice. Add bananas and stir gently. Cook at **MEDIUM** 1 minute.
Spoon warm bananas and sauce into dessert dishes. Top with whipped cream and sprinkle with toasted coconut.

## DIRECTIONS FOR COOKING MEAT

**General Directions:** For best results, select roasts that are uniform in shape.
Season as desired, but salt after cooking.
Browning sauce mixed with equal parts of butter will enhance the color.
Place meat on microwave roasting rack set in a 11 x 7-inch dish. Beef Rib Roast should be placed cut-side down. Other roasts and hams should be placed fat-side up. For **beef and lamb roasts,** loosely cover baking dish with wax paper to prevent spatter. For **pork roast**, cover with plastic wrap or place in oven cooking bag. See pork roast section below. If a large amount of juice accumulates in the bottom of the dish, drain occasionally. If desired, reserve for making gravy.

**Beef, Pork and Lamb Roasts:** Can be shielded at the beginning of cooking or halfway through cooking. If you wish to shield at the beginning of cooking, remove foil halfway through the cooking time. Beef and pork rib roasts should be shielded by the bones. Foil should extend about 2-inches down from bones. The shank bone on a lamb roast should be cupped with foil. Thin ends of boneless roasts should also be shielded. Foil should NOT touch oven sides since arcing may occur.

**Pork Roasts:** Cook, covered with plastic wrap, or in an oven cooking bag for best results. Prepare bag according to manufacturer's package directions. Do NOT use wire or metal twist-tie to close bag. Use nylon tie provided, or a piece of cotton string or a strip cut from the open end of the bag. Make six ½-inch slits by the closure to allow steam to escape.

**Hams:** Shield by wrapping a 3-inch wide strip of foil around the large end of the ham. Secure to the body of the ham with wooden toothpicks. Fold 1½-inches over cut surface. For shank ham halves shield shank bone by cupping it with foil. Place fat-side down. Cover with plastic wrap. One-third of the way through cooking, remove ham from oven and cut off skin. Turn fat-side up and reshield edges. If desired, glaze during last 10 to 20 minutes of cooking.

**Canned Hams:** Shield on the top cut-edge with a 1½-inch strip of foil. Wrap strip of foil around ham and secure to body of ham with wooden toothpicks. Fold 1-inch over cut surface. Cover with plastic wrap. Turn ham over and reshield, halfway through cooking. If desired, glaze during last 10 to 20 minutes of cooking.

**Pot Roasts** (2½ to 3½ pounds): Cook in liquid. Use 1½ cups of soup, broth, etc. Use an oven cooking bag or covered casserole when cooking less tender cuts of meat. Select a covered casserole dish deep enough so that the meat does not touch the lid. If an oven cooking bag is used, prepare the bag according to package directions. Do NOT use wire or metal twist-ties. Use the nylon tie provided or use a piece of cotton string or a strip cut from the open end of the bag. Make six ½-inch slits by the closure to allow steam to escape.

**Pork and Lamb Chops:** Arrange in a single layer with meatier portions toward edge of the dish.

**TO COOK BY TIME:** Multiply the weight of the roast by the minimum recommended minutes per pound. Program Power and Time. Turn roast over halfway through cooking.

**TO COOK BY EASY·MATIC TEMPERATURE PROBE or PROGRAMMABLE TEMPERATURE PROBE:** Insert probe into meat as horizontally as possible. Probe tip should be in center of meat, but not touching bone or fatty area. Set temperature as indicated in recipe or chart on page 22. When temperature in display window reaches 100°F, remove probe from meat without disconnecting from oven wall. Turn roast over and reinsert probe into a new position.

**After Cooking:** Check temperature using a meat thermometer. The thermometer should NOT touch bone or fat. If it does, the reading could be inaccurate. Lower temperatures are found in the center of the roast and in the muscle close to a large bone, such as a pork loin center rib roast. If the temperatures are low, return meat to the oven and cook a few more minutes at the recommended power level. **Do NOT use a conventional meat thermometer in the microwave oven.** Let stand, tented with foil, 10 to 15 minutes. During stand time internal temperature rises 5°F. to 15°F.

## MEAT ROASTING CHART FOR TIME COOKING

| MEAT | POWER | COOKING TIME | TEMPERATURE AFTER COOKING |
|---|---|---|---|
| **BEEF ROASTS** | | | |
| Rib, Boneless Rib, Top Sirloin | | | |
| Rare | MEDIUM-LOW | 11 to 12½ min./lb. | 120°F |
| Medium | MEDIUM-LOW | 13 to 14½ min./lb. | 130°F |
| Well | MEDIUM-LOW | 15 to 17 min./lb. | 160°F |
| Rump, Eye of Round (High Quality) | | | |
| Rare | MEDIUM-LOW | 7 to 8½ min./lb. | 110°F |
| Medium | MEDIUM-LOW | 11 to 12½ min./lb. | 120°F |
| Well | MEDIUM-LOW | 16½ to 21 min./lb. | 160°F |
| Pot Roast (2½ to 3½ lb.) Chunk, Rump. Turn meat over after 1 hour of cooking | LOW | 25 to 30 min./lb. | — |
| **PORK POASTS** | | | |
| Bone-in (Cover with plastic wrap) | MEDIUM-LOW | 14 to 16 min./lb. | 170°F |
| Boneless (Cover with plastic wrap) | MEDIUM-LOW | 13 to 14 min./lb. | 170°F |
| **HAM** (fully cooked) | | | |
| Canned (3 lb.) (Cover with plastic wrap) | MEDIUM-LOW | 9 to 9½ min./lb. | 120°F |
| Butt (Cover with plastic wrap) | MEDIUM-LOW | 11½ to 12 min./lb. | 120°F |
| Shank (8 lb.) (Cover with plastic wrap) | MEDIUM-LOW | 11 to 13 min./lb. | 120°F |
| **LAMB ROASTS** | | | |
| Bone-in | | | |
| Medium | MEDIUM-LOW | 12½ to 13 min./lb. | 140°F |
| Well | MEDIUM-LOW | 15 to 16½ min./lb. | 160°F |
| Boneless | | | |
| Medium | MEDIUM-LOW | 12½ to 13 min./lb. | 140°F |
| Well | MEDIUM-LOW | 13½ to 16 min./lb. | 160°F |

## MEAT ROASTING CHART FOR TEMPERATURE PROBE COOKING

| MEAT | EASY-MATIC TEMP | PROGRAMMABLE TEMPERATURE | | APPROXIMATE TEMPERATURE AFTER STANDING |
|---|---|---|---|---|
| | | FIRST—STAGE POWER & TEMP | SECOND-STAGE POWER & TEMP | |
| **Beef Roasts** (up to 5 lb.) | | | | |
| Rare | 1 | MEDIUM-LOW-100°F | LOW-120°F | 130°F to 145°F |
| Medium | 2 | MEDIUM-LOW-100°F | LOW-140°F | 145°F to 155°F |
| Well | 3 | MEDIUM-LOW-100°F | LOW-160°F | 160°F to 175°F |
| **Pork** Roast (up to 5 lb.) (Cover with plastic wrap) | 6 | MEDIUM-LOW-100°F | LOW -170°F | 170°F to 180°F |
| **Ham** (fully cooked) | | | | |
| Canned (3 to 5 lb.) (Cover with plastic wrap) | — | MEDIUM-LOW-100°F | LOW-120°F | 120°F to 130°F |
| Shank (8 lb.) (Cover with plastic wrap) | | MEDIUM-LOW-100°F | LOW-120°F | 120°F to 130°F |
| **Lamb Roast** (up to 5 lb.) | | | | |
| Medium | 4 | MEDIUM-LOW-100°F | LOW-140°F | 150°F to 160°F |
| Well | 5 | MEDIUM-LOW-100°F | LOW-160°F | 170°F to 180°F |

## DIRECTIONS FOR COOKING CONVENIENCE MEATS BY MICROWAVE

**Brush hamburgers** and **fresh sausage** links with browning sauce mixed with equal parts melted butter to enhance appearance.

**Pierce** sausage links and frankfurters with fork or **score** before cooking.

**Arrange food in** single layer in baking dish. Loosely cover with wax paper to prevent spatter.

**Place up to four slices of bacon** between layers of paper towels on paper plates.

**Let stand** according to recommended time in chart.

## DIRECTIONS FOR COOKING CONVENIENCE MEATS

| MEAT | AMOUNT | POWER | APPROX. COOKING TIME (in minutes) | STAND TIME (in minutes) |
|---|---|---|---|---|
| **Beef Patties,** frozen (3½ oz. ea.) | 1<br>2<br>4 | MEDIUM | 4 to 4½<br>6 to 7<br>9 to 11 | 2<br>3<br>3 |
| **Bacon Slices** | 2<br>3<br>4<br>8 | HIGH | 1½ to 2<br>2 to 2½<br>2½ to 3½<br>5 to 7 | 1<br>1<br>1<br>1 |
| **Canadian Bacon,** Slices (1 oz.) | 2<br>4<br>8 | HIGH | 1 to 1½<br>2 to 3<br>3 to 4 | 1<br>1<br>1 |
| **Frankfurters,** scored | 2<br>4 | MEDIUM | 1½ to 2<br>2½ to 3 | 2<br>2 |
| **Ham,** Slices (about 2 oz. ea.) | 2<br>4 | HIGH | 1½ to 2½<br>3½ to 4½ | 3<br>3 |
| **Hamburgers** (4 oz. ea.) | 1<br>2<br>4 | MEDIUM | 3 to 3½<br>4½ to 5<br>6½ to 7½ | 2<br>2<br>2 |
| **Lamb Chops,** shoulder, ¾-inch thick | 2 (about ¾ lb.)<br>4 (about 1½ lb.) | MEDIUM | 5½ to 7<br>10½ to 12 | 5<br>5 |
| **Pork Chops,** rib or loin, ½-inch thick | 2 (about ½ lb.)<br>4 (about 1 lb.) | MEDIUM | 5 to 6<br>8 to 10 | 5<br>5 |
| **Sausage Links,** frozen (precooked, brown and serve) | 2<br>4<br>8 | HIGH | 1 to 1½<br>1½ to 2<br>3 to 4 | 2<br>2<br>2 |
| **Sausage Links,** fresh (1 to 2 oz. ea.) | 2<br>4<br>8 | HIGH | 1 to 1½<br>1½ to 2½<br>3 to 4 | 3<br>3<br>3 |
| **Sausage Links** or **Patties** frozen, uncooked (1 to 2 oz. ea.) | 2<br>4 | HIGH | 1½ to 2½<br>2½ to 3½ | 2<br>2 |

## BEEF WITH BROCCOLI

**1 tablespoon oil**
**3/4 pound boneless steak, cut into thin strips**
**1 clove garlic, finely chopped**
**1/8 teaspoon ginger**
**1 1/2 cups broccoli flowerets**
**1 tablespoon cornstarch**
**1/2 cup beef broth**
**1 tablespoon sherry**
**1 tablespoon soy sauce**
**Toasted sesame seeds (see page 48)**

**Yield:** 4 Servings

Heat oil in 8-inch square dish at **HIGH** 2 minues. Stir in beef, garlic and ginger. Cook at **HIGH** 3 to 4 minutes. Stir twice. Add broccoli. Cover with plastic wrap. Cook at **HIGH** 3 to 5 minutes, or until broccoli is crisp-tender. Stir once. Blend cornstarch with broth, sherry, and soy sauce until smooth. Stir into beef mixture. Cook at **HIGH** 3 to 4 minutes, or until sauce is thickened. Stir once. Top with sesame seeds.

## TERIYAKI BEEF KABOBS

**2 tablespoons packed brown sugar**
**2 tablespoons soy sauce**
**1 tablespoon lemon juice**
**1 tablespoon oil**
**1 pound boneless beef steak, cut in 1 1/2-inch cubes**
**1/2 pint cherry tomatoes**
**1 medium green pepper, cut into chunks**

**Yield:** 4 Servings

In 1 1/2-quart bowl, combine sugar, soy sauce, lemon juice and oil; add steak. If desired, cover and marinate in refrigerator 3 hours. Stir occasionally.
On four 9 or 10-inch wooden skewers, alternately thread steak, tomatoes and green peppers. Lay skewers across an 8-inch square dish. Cook at **HIGH** 6 to 7 minutes*. Rearrange kabobs halfway through cooking.
*Cooking time given is for beef Medium-Rare. Adjust time accordinly for desired doneness.

## FLANK STEAK FLORENTINE

**1/4 pound fresh mushrooms**
**1 large onion, finely chopped**
**1 clove garlic, finely chopped**
**3 tablespoons butter or margarine, softened**
**1 package (10 oz.) frozen chopped spinach, defrosted and well drained (see page 9)**
**1 1/2 to 1 3/4 pound beef flank steak**
**2 beef bouillon cubes**
**1 cup hot water**
**1 can (10 3/4 oz.) condensed golden mushroom soup**
**2 tablespoons dry vermouth, optional**

**Yield:** 4 Servings

Chop 1/2 cup mushrooms. In medium bowl, combine chopped mushrooms, onions, garlic, butter and spinach. Cook at **HIGH** 3 to 4 minutes. Pound flank steak with mallet; score one side. Spread spinach mixture on steak in a lengthwise strip. Roll steak lengthwise around filling; tie with string or secure with wooden toothpick.
Place steak rolls in 10-inch square dish seam-side down. Combine bouillon, water, soup and vermouth; add remaining mushrooms, sliced. Pour sauce over steak roll. Cover with plastic wrap. Cook at **HIGH** 10 minutes and at **LOW** 20 to 25 minutes. Beef should be tender. Let stand, covered, 10 minutes before serving.

## BEST BEEF GOULASH

**2 pounds boneless beef, cut into 1-inch cubes**
**2 1/4 cups water, divided**
**1 envelope (1 3/8 oz.) onion soup mix**
**1 can (4 oz.) whole mushrooms, drained**
**2 tablespoons paprika**
**1/4 teaspoon caraway seeds**
**3 tablespoons cornstarch**

**Yield:** 6—8 Servings

In 4-quart casserole, combine beef, 2 cups water, onion soup mix, mushrooms, paprika and caraway seeds. Cover with lid. Cook at **HIGH** 10 minutes and at **LOW** 55 to 60 minutes; stir twice. Blend cornstarch with remaining 1/4 cup water until smooth. Stir into dish. Cook, uncovered, at **HIGH** 3 to 4 minutes, or until thickened.

## PEPPER STEAK

**2 tablespoons oil**
**1 pound boneless steak, cut into thin strips**
**2 tablespoons soy sauce**
**Dash ginger**
**Salt to taste**
**2 medium green peppers, cut into chunks**
**2 medium onions, sliced**
**1 tablespoon cornstarch**
**1/2 cup beef broth**

**Yield:** 4 Servings

Heat oil in 8-inch square dish at **HIGH** 4 minutes. Add steak, soy sauce and ginger. Cook at **HIGH** 7 to 8 minutes; stir once. Season with salt and stir in peppers and onions. Cover with plastic wrap. Cook at **HIGH** 3 to 4 minutes, or until vegetables are crisp-tender.
Blend cornstarch with broth until smooth. Stir into dish. Cook at **HIGH** 3 to 4 minutes, or until sauce is thickened; stir once.

## SWISS POT ROAST

**3 pounds boneless beef chuck steak (2 1/2-inch thick)**
**3 medium onions, sliced**
**2 carrots, sliced**
**2 green peppers, sliced**
**2 celery stalks, sliced**
**1 can (14.5 to 16 oz.) stewed tomatoes**
**2 packages instant beef broth**
**2 tablespoons packed brown sugar**
**1 teaspoon garlic powder**
**1/2 teaspoon salt**
**2 bay leaves**

**Yield:** 6—8 Servings

In 4-quart casserole combine all ingredients. Cover with lid. Cook at **HIGH** 15 minutes and at **LOW** 80 to 90 minutes, or until meat is fork-tender. Turn meat over and stir halfway through. Skim excess fat. Slice and serve immediately.

## BEEF STEW

**2 pounds boneless beef, cut into 1-inch cubes**
**2 cups water, divided**
**1 envelope (1 3/4 oz.) onion soup mix**
**4 medium carrots, thinly sliced**
**2 potatoes (about 8 oz. ea.) peeled and cut into 1/2-inch cubes**
**1 bay leaf**
**1 can (8 oz.) green peas, drained**
**1/4 cup flour**

**Yield:** 8 Servings

In 4-quart casserole, combine beef, 1 1/2 cups water, soup mix, carrots, potatoes and bay leaf. Cover with lid. Cook at **HIGH** 8 minutes and at **MEDIUM-LOW** 55 to 65 minutes, or until tender. Stir occasionally. Add peas. Blend flour with remaining 1/2 cup water. Add to stew. Cook at **HIGH** 5 to 7 minutes, or until stew is thickened, stir occasionally. Remove bay leaf before serving.

## HEAVENLY FRENCH DIP

**1 medium onion, cut into rings**
**2 tablespoons butter or margarine**
**1/2 loaf French bread (about 12 in. long)**
**1/4 to 1/3 pound slice cooked roast beef**
**Salt and pepper to taste**
**1 can (10 1/4 oz.) beef gravy**
**2 tablespoons red wine, optional**

**Yield:** 2 Servings

Combine onion and butter in small glass bowl. Cover with plastic wrap. Cook at **HIGH** 2 to 3 minutes, or until onion is tender; stir once. Meanwhile, slice bread in half lengthwise and then crosswise, forming 2 sandwiches. Arrange beef on 2 pieces of bread; top with onions, then season with salt and pepper. Close sandwich; wrap individually in paper napkins. In same glass bowl, combine gravy and wine. Cook at **HIGH** 2 1/2 to 3 1/2 minutes, or until heated through; stir once. Cook sandwiches at **MEDIUM** 1 1/2 to 2 minutes, or until warm. Serve with gravy for dipping.

## MIDGET MEAT LOAF

**1 pound ground beef**
**1 egg**
**1/3 cup dry bread crumbs**
**1/3 cup catsup**
**2 tablespoons milk or water**
**1 envelope (1/4 oz.) instant onion soup**

**Yield:** 4 Servings

Combine all ingredients. In 8-inch square dish, shape beef mixture into loaf. Cook at **MEDIUM** 14 to 16 minutes. Drain liquid occasionally. If necessary, shield ends of loaf with aluminum foil halfway through cooking. Let stand, covered, 5 minutes before serving.

***Note: For TWO Servings,*** *follow above procedure using 1/2 pound ground beef, 1 egg, 1/4 cup bread crumbs, 2 tablespoons catsup and 1 envelope instant onion soup. Shape into two loaves. Cook 6 to 8 minutes.*

## STUFFED GREEN PEPPERS

**1/2 pound ground beef**
**1 small onion, chopped**
**1 can (8 oz.) tomato sauce, divided**
**2 tablespoons water**
**2 tablespoons grated Parmesan cheese, divided**
**1/2 teaspoon salt**
**1/8 teaspoon pepper**
**1/4 cup instant rice**
**2 medium green peppers**

**Yield:** 2 Servings

Crumble ground beef into medium bowl. Add onion. Cook at **HIGH** 3 to 4 minutes, or until beef is browned; stir once. Drain. Stir in 1/2 can tomato sauce, water, 1 tablespoon cheese, salt and pepper. Cover with wax paper. Cook at **HIGH** 3 to 4 minutes. Stir in rice; let stand, covered, 5 minutes.

Meanwhile, cut peppers in half lengthwise; remove seeds and rinse. Spoon beef-rice filling into each half. Place in 8-inch square dish. Top with remaining sauce and cheese. Cover with wax paper. Cook at **HIGH** 8 to 10 minutes, or until peppers are tender. Let stand, covered, 5 minutes before serving.

## SWEDISH MEATBALLS

**1 pound ground beef**
**1 egg**
**1/2 cup dry bread crumbs**
**1/2 cup milk, divided**
**1 small onion, finely chopped**
**2 teaspoons parsley flakes**
**1/2 teaspoon salt**
**1/8 teaspoon allspice**
**1/8 teaspoon pepper**
**1 can (10 3/4 oz.) condensed golden mushroom soup**

**Yield:** 4 Servings

Combine ground beef, egg, bread crumbs, 1/4 cup milk, onion, parsley, salt, allspice and pepper. Shape into 1 1/4-inch meatballs (about 20). Arrange in 8-inch square dish. Cover with wax paper. Cook at **MEDIUM** 9 to 10 minutes. In small bowl, blend soup and remaining milk; combine with meatballs. Cook, covered, at **HIGH** 4 to 10 minutes, or until heated through. Serve, if desired, over buttered noodles, sprinkled with additional parsley.

## SALISBURY STEAK

**1 pound ground beef**
**1 can (10 3/4 oz.) condensed golden mushroom soup, divided**
**1 egg**
**1/3 cup bread crumbs**
**1 small onion, finely chopped**
**1/8 teaspoon pepper**
**1/2 cup milk**
**1 can (4 oz.) sliced mushrooms, drained**

**Yield:** 4 Servings

Combine ground beef, 1/4 cup soup, egg, bread crumbs, onion and pepper. Shape into 4 patties. Arrange in 8-inch square dish. Cover with wax paper. Cook at **HIGH** 8 to 10 minutes. Turn patties over halfway through cooking. Drain and let stand 5 minutes.

Meanwhile, in small glass bowl, combine remaining soup, milk and mushrooms. Cook at **HIGH** 3 to 5 minutes, or until hot; stir once. Pour sauce over patties. Serve immediately.

## CHILI

**1 pound lean ground beef**
**2 medium onions, chopped**
**1/4 teaspoon dried garlic pieces**
**1 can (16 oz.) pinto or red kidney beans**
**1 can (14.5 to 16 oz.) stewed tomatoes, chopped**
**1 can (15 oz.) tomato sauce**
**1 teaspoon salt**
**2 to 3 tablespoons chili powder**

**Yield:** 4 Servings

Crumble ground beef in 3-quart casserole. Stir in onions and garlic. Cook at **HIGH** 6 to 7 minutes. Stir once; drain. Stir in remaining ingredients. Cover with lid. Cook at **HIGH** 10 minutes and at **MEDIUM-LOW** 35 to 40 minutes; stir occasionally. Let stand, covered, 7 minutes before serving.

## SLOPPY JOES

**1 pound ground beef**
**1 large onion, finely chopped**
**1/2 to 3/4 cup catsup**
**1/4 cup sweet pickled relish**
**Salt and pepper to taste**
**4 hamburger rolls**

**Yield:** 4 Servings

Crumble ground beef in 2-quart casserole. Stir in onion. Cook at **HIGH** 4 to 5 minutes, or until beef is browned. Stir once; drain. Stir in catsup, relish, salt and pepper. Cover with lid. Cook at **HIGH** 2 minutes and at **MEDIUM** 3 to 4 minutes. Stir once. Serve in split hamburger rolls.

***Variation:*** *Add 1/2 pound frankfurters, sliced, with ground beef.*

## ORIENTAL PEPPER BURGERS

**1 pound ground beef**
**1/4 teaspoon salt**
**1/8 teaspoon pepper**
**1 large onion, sliced**
**1 medium green pepper, cut into chunks**
**1 can (8 oz.) tomato sauce**
**1/4 teaspoon ginger**
**4 teaspoons soy sauce**

**Yield:** 4 Servings

Combine beef, salt and pepper; shape into 4 patties and arrange in 12x8-inch dish. Cook at **MEDIUM-HIGH** 4 1/2 to 5 1/2 minutes; drain. Add onion, green pepper and tomato sauce blended with ginger and soy sauce. Cover with plastic wrap. Cook at **MEDIUM-HIGH** 5 1/2 to 6 1/2 minutes, or until vegetables are tender. Let stand, covered, 5 minutes before serving.

## FIREHOUSE CHILI

**1 tablespoon oil**
**1 large onion, chopped**
**1 clove garlic, finely chopped**
**1 1/2 pounds beef round steak, cut into 1/2-inch cubes**
**1/2 stick pepperoni (about 4 oz.), sliced into 1/4-inch slices, then quartered.**
**2 tablespoons flour**
**1/2 to 1 tablespoon chili powder**
**1 can (14 1/2 oz.) whole tomatoes, chopped**
**1 beef bouillon cube, crushed**
**1 bay leaf**
**1/2 teaspoon oregano**
**1/2 teaspoon salt**
**1/4 to 1/2 teaspoon ground cumin**
**1/4 to 1/2 teaspoon red pepper**
**1 medium green pepper, cut into 1/2-inch cubes**
**1 can (16 oz.) kidney beans, drained**
**1 package (10 oz.) frozen corn, defrosted and drained (see page 9)**

**Yield:** 5—6 Servings

In 3-quart casserole, combine oil, onion and garlic. Cook at **HIGH** 2 to 3 minutes, or until onion is tender; stir once. Add beef and pepperoni to onion mixture. Combine flour and chili powder; stir into meat and mix well. Add tomatoes, bouillon, bay leaf, oregano, salt, cumin and red pepper; mix well.

**TO COOK BY TEMPERATURE:** Position probe in center of dish. Cover with lid. Set Easy Matic TEMP 8. After selected temperature is reached, oven will automatically hold at 190°F for 2 1/2 hours. Stir occasionally. Add green pepper, kidney beans and corn 20 minutes from end of cooking. Remove bay leaf before serving.

**TO COOK BY TIME:** Cover with lid. Cook at **HIGH** 20 minutes and **LOW** 60 minutes; stir three times. Stir in green pepper, kidney beans and corn. Cook, covered, at **LOW** 15 to 20 minutes, or until peppers are tender-crisp. Remove bay leaf. Serve with crackers.

## APPLE-STUFFED PORK CHOPS

**4 rib pork chops, 1-inch thick**
**1/4 cup butter or margarine, melted**
**1/2 cup chopped apple**
**1/2 cup herb-seasoned stuffing mix**
**1/4 cup (1 oz.) shredded Cheddar cheese**
**2 tablespoons chopped celery**
**1 tablespoon chopped onion**
**1 tablespoon chopped raisins**
**2 tablespoons orange juice**
**1/4 teaspoon salt**

**Yield:** 4 Servings

Cut pocket in each chop. In bowl, combine butter, apples, stuffing mix, cheese, celery, onion, raisins, orange juice and salt; mix well. Fill each pocket with stuffing; secure opening with wooden toothpicks.
Arrange pork chops in 12x8-inch dish. Cover with wax paper. Cook at **MEDIUM** 17 to 19 minutes. Let stand, covered, 5 minutes. Place remaining stuffing in bowl. Cover with plastic wrap. Cook at **MEDIUM** 2 to 3 minutes, or until hot.

## CHINESE PORK AND GREEN VEGETABLES

**1 pound boneless pork, cut into thin strips**
**2 tablespoons soy sauce**
**1/8 teaspoon garlic powder**
**1 package (6 oz.) frozen pea pods, defrosted (see page 9)**
**2 bunches green onions, cut into 3/4-inch pieces**
**1 1/2 to 2 tablespoons cornstarch**
**1 cup beef broth**

**Yield:** 4 Servings

In 8-inch square dish, combine pork, soy sauce and garlic. Cook at **MEDIUM-HIGH** 4 to 5 minutes; stir occasionally. Add pea pods and green onions: Cover with plastic wrap. Cook at **MEDIUM-HIGH** 3 minutes, or until pork is tender; stir once. Blend cornstarch with broth until smooth. Stir into pork mixture. Cook at **MEDIUM-HIGH** 4 minutes, or until sauce is slightly thickened; stir occasionally. Serve, if desired, over rice.

## SWEET AND SOUR PORK

**1 can (8 1/4 oz.) chunk pineapple in heavy syrup, drained; reserve 1/3 cup syrup**
**1/4 cup white vinegar**
**1 tablespoon cornstarch**
**2 tablespoons oil**
**1 pound boneless pork, cut into 3/4-inch cubes**
**1/4 cup soy sauce**
**1 bunch green onions, thinly sliced**
**1 green pepper, cut into small chunks**

**Yield:** 4 Servings

In small glass bowl, combine reserved syrup, vinegar and cornstarch. Cook at **HIGH** 3/4 to 1 minutes, or until thickened; stir once.
Place oil in 8-inch square dish. Cook at **HIGH** 2 minutes; stir in pork, soy sauce and onions. Cook at **HIGH** 7 to 8 minutes; stir twice. Add green pepper and pineapple. Cover with plastic wrap. Cook at **HIGH** 2 to 3 minutes, or until pork is tender.
Stir in sauce and let stand, covered, 5 minutes.

## OVEN-FRIED PORK CHOPS

**6 rib pork chops, 1/2-inch thick**
**1 package (1 3/8 oz.) seasoned coating mix for pork**

**Yield:** 6 Servings

Coat chops as package directs. Line 12x8-inch dish with paper towel; arrange chops, ribs toward center. Cover with wax paper. Cook at **MEDIUM** 15 to 17 minutes. Let stand, uncovered, 5 minutes before serving.

## SOUTHERN BARBECUED RIBS

**1 rack (2 to 3 lb.) pork spareribs**
**1 cup water**
**1 cup barbecue sauce**
**2 tablespoons honey or dark corn syrup**
**2 tablespoons flour**
**1 tablespoon soy sauce**

**Yield:** 4 Servings

Place ribs and water in 12x8-inch dish. Cover with plastic wrap. Cook at **HIGH** 20 minutes.
Remove ribs; discard water. Place ribs, meat-side down in same 12x8-inch dish. Combine remaining ingredients; pour over ribs. Cook at **MEDIUM-LOW** 30 to 40 minutes, or until tender. Turn over halfway through cooking; baste occasionally.

## KIELBASA 'N BEER CASSEROLE

**3 slices bacon, cut into 1-inch pieces**
**1 large onion, chopped**
**1 tablespoon flour**
**1 pound Kielbasa sausage, cut into 1-inch pieces**
**1 large carrot, shredded**
**1 can (12 oz.) beer**
**1/4 teaspoon pepper**
**1 can (16 oz.) sauerkraut, well drained**

**Yield:** 4 Servings

Place bacon in 3-quart casserole. Cook at **HIGH** 2 1/2 minutes, stir once. Add onion. Cook at **HIGH** 2 1/2 minutes; stir once. Stir in flour. Add Kielbasa, carrots, beer and pepper.
Cook at **HIGH** 8 minutes; stir twice. Stir in sauerkraut. Cook at **HIGH** 2 1/2 to 3 minutes, or until heated through.

## HAM STEAK WITH RAISIN SAUCE

**1/2 cup water**
**1/3 cup raisins**
**1/3 cup currant jelly**
**1/2 teaspoon grated orange peel**
**Dash allspice**
**1 tablespoon cornstarch**
**1/3 cup orange juice**
**1 pound ham steak (1-inch thick)**

**Yield:** 4 Servings

In glass bowl, combine water, raisins, jelly, orange peel and allspice. Cook at **HIGH** 3 to 4 minutes; stir once. Blend cornstarch with orange juice until smooth. Stir into sauce. Cook at **HIGH** 1 minute, or until sauce is thickened; stir once. Cook ham in 8-inch square dish at **HIGH** 6 to 7 minutes; turn ham over. Pour raisin sauce over ham; cook at **HIGH** 1 minute. Let stand, covered, 5 minutes before serving.

## COUNTRY HAM CASSEROLE

**1 package (8 oz.) noodles**
**1 can (10 3/4 oz.) condensed cream of celery soup**
**3/4 cup milk**
**1/2 teaspoon dry mustard, optional**
**2 cups cut-up cooked ham (about 3/4 lb.)**
**1 1/2 cups (6 oz.) shredded Swiss cheese, divided**
**1 can (16 oz.) green peas, drained**
**French fried onion pieces or crushed corn chips**

**Yield:** 4 Servings

Cook noodles according to directions on page 30. In 3-quart casserole, combine soup, milk and mustard. Stir in noodles, ham, 1 1/4 cups cheese, and peas. Cover with lid. Cook at **HIGH** 12 to 14 minutes. Stir twice. Top with remaining cheese and onion pieces. Let stand, covered, 5 minutes before serving.

## SHEPHERD'S PIE

**1 large onion, chopped**
**3 tablespoons butter or margarine**
**1/2 tablespoon parsley flakes**
**1 1/2 cups beef gravy**
**2 cups cut-up cooked lamb or beef (about 3/4-inch pieces)**
**1 package (10 oz.) frozen peas and carrots**
**1 1/2 to 2 cups hot mashed potatoes (see page 44)**
**Paprika**

**Yield:** 4 Servings

Combine onion and butter in 2-quart casserole. Cook at **HIGH** 2 to 2 1/2 minutes, or until onion is tender. Stir in parsley; gradually add gravy. Cook at **HIGH** 3 to 4 minutes, or until gravy is hot; stir twice. Stir in lamb, peas and carrots. Cook at **HIGH** 6 to 8 minutes, or until heated through; stir twice. Spoon potatoes on top of casserole; sprinkle with paprika. Cook at **HIGH** 1 1/2 to 2 minutes.

## IRISH STEW

**2 pounds boneless lamb, cut into 1-inch cubes**
**2 medium carrots, sliced into 1/4-inch pieces**
**2 potatoes ( about 6 oz. ea.), peeled and cubed**
**2 1/2 cups hot water, divided**
**1 envelope (1 oz.) onion-mushroom soup mix**
**1 bay leaf**
**1/4 cup flour**

**Yield:** 8 Servings

In 4-quart casserole, arrange lamb, carrots and potatoes, forming three separate layers. In bowl, combine 2 cups hot water, onion-mushroom mix and bay leaf. Stir together until well blended. Pour mixture over potatoes. Cover with lid. Cook at **HIGH** 10 minutes and at **LOW** 70 to 75 minutes. Stir twice. Blend flour with remaining 1/2 cup water until smooth. Stir into dish.* Cook at **HIGH** 4 to 5 minutes, or until stew is thickened. Remove bay leaf before serving.

*If desired, add 1/4 teaspoon browning sauce.

## GREEK LAMB CHOPS

**1/4 cup dry red wine**
**4 shoulder lamb chops, 3/4-inch thick**
**2 cloves garlic, chopped**
**3/4 teaspoon oregano**
**3/4 teaspoon coarsely ground pepper**
**Dash salt**

**Yield:** 4 Servings

Pour wine into 12x8-inch dish; add chops, turning to coat with wine. Sprinkle with remaining ingredients. Cover with wax paper. Cook at **MEDIUM** 9 to 11 minutes. Let stand, covered, 2 minutes.

## PASTA, RICE AND CEREAL CHART

| ITEM | CONTAINER | AMOUNT OF WATER | POWER TO COOK | APPROX. TIME TO COOK (in minutes) | STAND. TIME (in minutes) | SPECIAL INSTRUCTIONS |
|---|---|---|---|---|---|---|
| **Pasta** | | **Boiling Water** | | | | Add 1 teaspoon oil to water. Cover and heat hot water to a boil (13 to 18 min.). Add pasta; stir. Cook uncovered; stir. Let stand, covered. Pasta that is to be added to a casserole should be slightly undercooked. |
| Egg Noodles medium width (8 oz.) | 3-qt casserole | 1 quart | HIGH | 9 to 10 | 3 | |
| Elbow Macaroni (8 oz.) | 3-qt casserole | 1½ quarts | HIGH | 13 to 18 | 3 | |
| Spaghetti (8 oz., broken) | 3-qt casserole | 2 quarts | HIGH | 17 to 19 | 3 | |
| **Rice*** | | **Boiling water** | | | | Cover and heat hot water to a boil (7 to 8 min.). Add rice, salt and butter (amount of salt and butter as package directs). Cook covered; stir. Let stand, covered. |
| Flavored Rice Mix (4.4 to 7.5 oz.) | 2-qt casserole | as package directs | M.LOW | 15 to 30 Check package time | 10 | |
| Long Grain (1 cup) | 2-qt casserole | 2 cups | M.LOW | 13½ to 15 | 10 | |
| Short Grain (1 cup) | 2-qt casselore | 2 cups | M.LOW | 10 to 12 | 10 | |
| **Cereal** Cream of Wheat (regular) | | **Boiling water** | | | | Cover and heat hot water to a boil (3 to 4 min.). Add cereal, cook uncovered. Stir once before stand. |
| 1 serving (2½ tbsps.) | 1 qt. glass bowl | 1 cup | LOW | 2 to 3½ | 1 | |
| 2 servings (⅓ cup) | 1½-qt glass bowl | 1¾ cups | LOW | 4 to 6 | 1 | |
| Farina | | **Boiling Water** | | | | Cover and heat hot water to a boil (3 to 4 min.). Slowly add cereal; stir continuously. Cook uncovered. Stir once before stand. |
| 1 serving (3 tbsps) | 1-qt glass bowl | 1 cup | LOW | 2 to 3 | 1 | |
| 2 servings (6 tbsps) | 1½-qt glass bowl | 2 cups | LOW | 4 to 5 | 1 | |
| Oatmeal | | **Hot water** | | | | Combine water and cereal. Cook uncovered. Stir once before stand. |
| 1 serving (⅓ cup) | individual serving dish | ½ cup | HIGH | 1 to 2 | 1 | |
| 2 servings (⅔ cup) | 1½-qt glass-bowl | 1½ cups | HIGH | 3 to 4 | 1 | |
| 4 servings (1⅓ cups) | 2-qt glass bowl | 3 cups | HIGH | 5 to 6 | 2 | |
| Wheat-Bran Cereal | | **Hot water** | | | | Combine water and cereal. Cook uncovered. Stir once before stand. |
| 1 serving (¼ cup) | 1-qt glass bowl | ¾ cup | HIGH | 3 to 4 | 1 | |
| 2 servings (½ cup) | 1½-qt glass bowl | 1½ cups | HIGH | 6 to 7½ | 1 | |
| 4 servings (1 cup) | 2-qt glass bowl | 3 cups | HIGH | 7 to 8 | 2 | |

*For instant rice products, use package directions. Bring hot water to a boil.

## PASTA PRIMAVERA

**1 package (8 oz.), rotelle pasta, or spaghetti, broken**
**2 cups broccoli flowerets**
**2 cups cauliflowerets**
**3 carrots, cut into sticks**
**2 cloves garlic, finely chopped**
**1/4 cup chopped fresh parsley**
**2 tablespoons oil**
**1 teaspoon basil**
**3 tablespoons butter or margarine**
**1/3 cup grated Parmesan cheese**
**Pepper to taste**

**Yield:** 4 Servings

Cook pasta according to chart, page 30. In 3-quart casserole, combine broccoli, cauliflower, carrots, garlic, parsley, oil and basil. Cover with lid. Cook at **HIGH** 5 to 7 minutes. Let stand, covered, 3 minutes.
Meanwhile, in medium glass bowl, heat butter at **HIGH** 1 to 1 1/2 minutes, or until melted; stir in drained pasta. Add vegetables and cheese; toss well. Season with pepper.

## FETTUCCINE ALFREDO

**1 package (8 oz.) fettuccine**
**1 cup grated Parmesan cheese**
**1/2 cup butter or margarine, cut into quarters**
**1/2 cup heavy cream**
**Pepper to taste**

**Yield:** 4 Side-Dish Servings

Cook fettuccine according to directions for egg noodles in chart, page 30. While noodles are standing, combine cheese, butter and cream in microwave-safe serving bowl. Cook at **MEDIUM** 3 to 4 minutes, or until butter is melted; stir twice. Stir in drained noodles; toss well. Season with pepper.

## FLORIDA-STYLE NOODLES

**1 package (8 oz.) medium egg noodles**
**1/2 cup almonds**
**1/4 cup butter or margarine**
**1 tablespoon poppy seeds**
**1/2 tablespoon grated lemon peel**
**1/2 tablespoon grated orange peel**
**1/2 teaspoon salt**
**1/8 teaspoon pepper**
**1 cup sour cream**

**Yield:** 4 Servings

Cook noodles according to chart, page 30. While noodles are standing, in microwave-safe serving bowl, combine almonds and butter. Heat at **HIGH** 1 to 1 1/2 minutes, or until butter is melted. Stir in drained noodles, poppy seeds, lemon and orange peel, salt and pepper; toss well. Serve with sour cream.

## RICE PILAF

**1/4 cup butter or margarine**
**1 cup long grain rice**
**2 1/4 cups chicken broth**
**1/4 cup raisins, optional**
**1 to 1 1/2 teaspoons curry powder**

**Yield:** 6 Servings

Heat butter in 2-quart casserole at **MEDIUM-LOW** 1 to 2 minutes, or until melted; stir in rice. Cook at **HIGH** 2 to 3 minutes, or until rice is browned; stir once. Add remaining ingredients. Cover with lid. Cook at **HIGH** 5 minutes and at **MEDIUM-LOW** 12 to 14 minutes, or until rice is tender. Let stand, covered, 5 minutes before serving.

***Variation:*** *Cook 1/4 cup slivered almonds with butter.*

## SPANISH RICE

**1 large onion, chopped**
**1/4 cup finely chopped green pepper**
**2 tablespoons butter or margarine**
**Water**
**1 can (14.5 to 16 oz.) stewed tomatoes, chopped and drained; reserve liquid**
**1 cup long grain rice**
**1 1/2 teaspoons salt**
**1/8 teaspoon pepper**

**Yield:** 6 Servings

In 2-quart casserole, combine onion, green pepper and butter. Cook at **HIGH** 2 1/2 to 3 1/2 minutes; stir once. Add enough water to reserved liquid to equal 2 cups. Add to dish with tomatoes, rice, salt and pepper. Cover with lid. Cook at **HIGH** 5 minutes and at **MEDIUM-LOW** 16 to 17 minutes, or until rice is tender; stir once. Let stand, covered, 5 minutes before serving.

## GRANOLA CEREAL

**2 cups quick or old-fashioned oats**
**2/3 cup soy nuts or coarsely chopped nut**
**1/3 cup wheat germ, optional**
**1/4 cup packed brown sugar**
**1/4 cup honey**
**1 teaspoon vanilla**
**1/3 cup raisins or coconut**

**Yield:** 3 Cups

Cook oats in 2-quart casserole at **HIGH** 3 to 5 minutes; stir occasionally. Add nuts, wheat germ, and brown sugar; stir in honey and vanilla. Cook at **HIGH** 3 to 5 minutes; stir twice. Add raisins. Cool completely, stirring occasionally to crumble mixture. Store in airtight container.

***Note:*** *To make **GRANOLA SNACK,** follow above procedure. Add 1/4 cup oil with honey.*

## PREPARING PIE CRUSTS

Prepare pastry according to recipe or package directions.

If desired, for a single crust homemade pastry recipe, substitute 1/2 cup whole wheat flour for 1/2 cup all- purpose flour.

Microwave pie crusts are light in color. A few drops of yellow food coloring may be mixed with the liquid before adding liquid to the flour mixture. This will give the crust a pale yellow color.

Roll dough out and gently place in pie plate.

Trim edge so a 3/4-inch overhang remains. Roll overhang down to rim of pie plate. Flute edge.

Prick bottom and sides of pastry with fork.

Let pie crust rest 10 minutes. This rest time helps reduce shrinkage.

If desired, brush with dark corn syrup or molasses for sweet fillings, or brush with Worcestershire or soy sauce for savory fillings.

**For frozen crust,** thaw and remove from foil pie plate and place in an 8 to 9-inch glass pie plate. Place on an inverted pie plate. Heat 15 seconds then prick crust and, if desired, brush with dark corn syrup, molasses, Worcestershire or soy sauce.

**For crumb crusts** combine 1/3 cup butter and 1/4 cup sugar in 9-inch pie plate. Heat 1 1/2 to 2 minutes, or untill butter is melted. Combine 1 1/4 cup crumbs (graham crackers, chocolate or vanilla wafers). Firmly pat into pie plate.

Cook according to directions given in chart. Rotate dish 1/4 turn halfway through cooking.
Visually check for doneness. Pastry crusts should be opaque. If crust is undercooked, add cooking time in 15 second increments.

Let stand until cool. Chill crumb crust.

### PIE CRUST CHART

| PIE CRUST | POWER | APPROXIMATE COOKING TIME (in minutes) |
|---|---|---|
| **Homemade or Mix** | **HIGH** | 4 to 5 |
| **Frozen** | **HIGH** | 4 to 5 |
| **Graham Cracker** or **Cookie Crumb** | **MEDIUM** | 2 to 2 1/2 |

## COCONUT LEMON MERINGUE PIE

**1 1/2 cups sugar**
**1/3 cup cornstarch**
**1/4 teaspoon salt**
**1 1/2 cups boiling water**
**3 eggs, separeated**
**1/2 cup lemon juice**
**3 tablespoons butter or margarine**
**Grated peel of 1 lemon**
**9-inch pie shell baked (see chart)**
**1/3 cup sugar**
**1/4 cup toasted coconut (see page 48)**

**Yield:** 8 Servings

In a 3-quart casserole, combine 1 1/2 cups sugar, cornstarch and salt; stir in boiling water. Cover with lid. Cook at **HIGH** 7 to 8 1/2 minutes, or until thickened; stir twice. Stir in small amount of hot mixture into egg yolks; return to hot mixture, beating until well blended. Add lemon juice, butter and lemon peel. Pour into pie shell; set aside. Meanwhile, beat egg whites until soft peaks form, gradually add remaining sugar and beat until stiff. Spread meringue over filling, making sure it touches crust all around. Sprinkle with coconut. Cook at **HIGH** 3 to 4 minutes, or until meringue is set. Cool completely.

## CHOCOLATE ROCKY ROAD PIE

**1 package (3 5/8 oz.) chocolate pudding and pie filling mix.**
**1 3/4 cups milk**
**1 to 1 1/2 cups miniature marshmallows**
**1/2 to 1 cup coarsely chopped walnuts**
**9-inch chocolate cookie crumb crust, baked (see chart)**

**Yield:** 8 Servings

Combine pudding mix and milk in 4-cup glass measure. Cook at **MEDIUM** 6 to 8 minutes, or until pudding is thickened; stir twice. Cool 5 minutes; fold in marshmallows and nuts. Turn into prepared crust; chill until firm.

## DIRECTIONS FOR ROASTING POULTRY

Season as desired, but salt after cooking. Browning sauce mixed with equal parts of butter will enhance the appearance.

Poultry may be stuffed or unstuffed. Tie legs together with cotton string. Place (breast-side up) on microwave roasting rack set in 11 x 7 inch dish or 12-inch round dish. Place poultry over 4 pounds breast-side down; turn over halfway through cooking. Cover with wax paper to prevent spatter. If desired, for a moister turkey, turkey breast or whole poultry, cover with plastic wrap.

Less tender hens should be cooked in liquid such as soup or broth. Use 1/4 cup per pound of poultry. Use an oven cooking bag or covered casserole. Select a covered casserole deep enough so that hen does not touch the lid.

If an oven cooking bag is used, prepare according to package directions, Do NOT use wire twist-ties to close bag. Do use nylon tie, a piece of cotton string or a strip cut from the open end of the bag. Make six 1/2-inch slits by the closure to allow steam to escape.

**TO COOK BY TIME:** Multiply the weight of the poultry by the minimum recommended minutes per pound. Program Power and Time.

**TO COOK BY TEMPERATURE PROBE:**
Cook poultry breast-side down according to the minutes per pound given in the chart below. Cover with wax paper or plastic wrap. Carefully turn poultry breast-side up. Insert temperature probe parallel to the leg into the thickest portion of the thigh. The probe should be between the inner thigh and body of the bird and should not touch bones. Recover. If it is necessary to shield the poultry during cooking, do NOT let foil touch the probe.

If a large amount of juice accumulates in the bottom of the baking dish, occasionally drain it. If desired, reserve for making gravy.

During cooking it may be necessary to shield legs, wings and the breast bone to prevent overcooking. Wooden toothpicks can be used to hold foil in place.
After cooking, check the temperature of large chickens and turkeys with a meat thermometer. Check the temperature in both thigh muscles. If thermometer touches bone, the reading may be inaccurate. **Do NOT use a conventional thermometer in the oven when cooking by microwave.** Small chickens and game birds are cooked when juices run clear and drumsticks readily move up and down. If poultry is undercooked, cook a few more minutes at the recommended power level. Let stand, tented with foil, 10 to 15 minutes before carving.

**TO COOK CHICKEN PARTS:** Arrange pieces skin-side up, with meatier portions toward edge of dish. Cover with wax paper. Multiply the weight by 7 1/2 to 8 1/2 minutes per pound. Cook at **HIGH**. Poultry is cooked when juices are clear. Let stand, covered, 5 minutes before serving.

## POULTRY CHART FOR TIME COOKING

| POULTRY | POWER | COOKING TIME (Minutes per Pound) | TEMPERATURE AFTER COOKING |
|---|---|---|---|
| **Cornish Hens** (1 to 1 1/2 lb. ea.) | HIGH | 7 1/2 to 9 1/2 | — |
| **Chicken** (up to 4 lb.) | HIGH | 8 1/2 to 9 1/2 | — |
| **Chicken** (4 to 6 lb.)* | MEDIUM | 10 1/2 to 11 1/2 | 190°F. |
| **Chicken Parts** | HIGH | 7 to 8 | — |
| **Turkey** (up to 12 lb.)* | MEDIUM | 11 to 13 | 190°F. |
| **Turkey Breast** (5 to 7 lb.) | MEDIUM-LOW | 14 to 15 | 170°F. |
| **Duck** (3 to 5 lb.) | MEDIUM | 9 1/2 to 11 | — |

*Start breast-side down. Turn over halfway through cooking.

## APRICOT-GLAZED CHICKEN

**2 pounds chicken parts**
**3/4 cup apricot preserves**
**1/2 cup bottled red Russian dressing**
**2 envelopes (1/4 oz. ea.) instand onion soup**

**Yield:** 4 Servings

Arrange chicken in 8-inch square dish, with meatier portions toward edge of dish. Cover with wax paper. Cook at **HIGH** 12 to 14 minutes, or until chicken is almost tender; drain. Combine remaining ingredients and spoon over chicken. Cook chicken, uncovered, at **MEDIUM** 5 to 5 1/2 minutes, or until chicken is glazed. Let stand 5 minutes before serving.

## CALIFORNIA CHICKEN

**2 chicken breasts, split (1 3/4 to 2 lb.)**
**2 teaspoons lemon juice**
**1 teaspoon onion flakes**
**Basil**
**Pepper**
**2/3 cup (2 2/3 oz.) shredded Cheddar cheese, divided**
**1/2 small avocado, thinly sliced**
**4 thin slices tomato**

**Yield:** 4 Servings

Arrange chicken in 8-inch square dish, with meatier portions toward edge of dish. Sprinkle with lemon juice, onion flakes, basil and pepper. Cover with wax paper. Cook at **HIGH** 12 to 15 minutes, or until chicken is tender. Top chicken with 1/3 cup cheese, avocado, tomato and remaining cheese. Cover with wax paper. Cook at **HIGH** 2 1/2 to 3 minutes.
Let stand, covered, 5 minutes before serving.

## CHICKEN CACCIATORE

**2 pounds chicken parts**
**1 can (15 oz.) tomato sauce**
**1 can (4 oz.) sliced mushrooms, drained**
**1 medium onion, chopped**
**1 tablespoon sugar, optional**
**1 tablespoon oregano**
**1 teaspoon salt**
**1 clove garlic, finely chopped**
**1/4 teaspoon pepper**

**Yield:** 2—3 Servings

Arrange chicken in 12x8-inch dish, with meatier portions toward edge of dish. Combine remaining ingredients; pour over chicken. Cover with wax paper. Cook at **HIGH** 20 to 22 minutes, or until chicken is tender. Halfway through cooking rearrange chicken. Let stand, covered, 5 minutes. Serve, if desired, with spaghetti.

## BARBECUED CHICKEN

**2 pounds chicken parts**
**3/4 cup barbecue sauce**

**Yield:** 2—3 Servings

Arrange chicken in 8-inch square dish with meatier portions toward edge of dish. Spread sauce evenly over chicken. Cover with wax paper. Cook at **HIGH** 14 to 16 minutes. Baste chicken with sauce. Cook, uncovered, at **HIGH** 3 to 5 minutes. Chicken should be tender. Let stand, covered, 5 minutes before serving.

## POULTRY ROASTING CHART FOR TEMPERATURE PROBE

| POULTRY | BREAST-SIDE DOWN | | BREAST-SIDE UP | | | |
|---|---|---|---|---|---|---|
| | | | EASY·MATIC TEMP | PROGRAMMABLE TEMP | | APPROX. TEMPERATURE AFTER STANDING |
| | POWER | MINUTES PER POUND | SETTING | FIRST STAGE POWER & TEMP | SECOND STAGE POWER & TEMP | |
| Chicken (4 to 7 lb.) | MEDIUM | 2 to 3 | TEMP 7 | MEDIUM-140°F | MEDIUM-LOW 180°F | 180°F to 190°F |
| Turkey (up to 8 lb.) | MEDIUM | 4 to 5 | TEMP 7 | MEDIUM-140°F | MEDIUM-LOW 180°F | 180°F to 190°F |

## BUTTERED BAKED CHICKEN

**2 pound chicken, cut into serving pieces**
**3 tablespoons butter or margarine, melted**
**1 teaspoon browning sauce**

**Yield:** 4 Servings

Arrange chicken in 8-inch square dish with meatier portions toward edge of dish. Combine butter and browning sauce. Brush half of butter mixture over chicken. Cover with wax paper. Cook at **HIGH** 16 to 18 minutes, or until chicken is done. Halfway through cooking, brush remaining butter mixture on chicken. Let stand, covered, 5 minutes before serving.

***Note: For TWO Servings,*** *follow above procedure. Halve all ingredients and cook 8 to 9 minutes.*
***For ONE Serving,*** *cook chicken 3½ to 5 minutes.*

## CHICKEN TERIYAKI

**2 pounds chicken parts**
**1 can (8 oz.) chunk pineapple in pineapple juice**
**1 clove garlic, finely chopped**
**¼ cup soy sauce**
**2 tablespoons packed brown sugar**
**½ teaspoon salt**
**¼ teaspoon ginger**

**Yield:** 4 Servings

Arrange chicken in 8-inch square dish with meatier portions toward the edge of dish. In small bowl, combine remaining ingredients; stir well. Pour sauce over chicken. Cover with wax paper. Cook at **HIGH** 16 to 18 minutes, or until chicken is tender. Let stand, covered, 5 minutes. To serve, spoon pineapple sauce over chicken.

## CHICKEN WITH SNOW PEAS

**4 chicken legs, thighs detached (12 lb.)**
**1 tablespoon butter or margarine, melted**
**1 tablespoon soy sauce**
**1½ teaspoons paprika**
**½ teaspoon crushed rosemary**
**¼ teaspoon salt**
**1 package (6 oz.) frozen pea pods, defrosted (see page 9)**
**1 can (4 oz.) sliced mushrooms, drained**

**Yield: 6** Servings

Arrange chicken in 12x8-inch dish. Combine butter, soy sauce, paprika, rosemary and salt; brush over chicken. Cover with wax paper. Cook at **HIGH** 13 to 15 minutes. Top with pea pods and mushrooms; cook, covered, at **HIGH** 5 to 7 minutes, or until chicken and vegetables are tender. Let stand, covered, 5 minutes before serving.

## CHICKEN'N SPINACH TOSS

**3 tablespoons soy sauce**
**2 tablespoons sherry**
**2 tablespoons water**
**1½ tablespoons Hoisin sauce**
**1 tablespoon cornstarch**
**½ tablespoon sugar**
**¼ teaspoon ginger**
**1 clove garlic, finely chopped**
**2 boneless chicken breasts, skinned, split and thinly sliced (about 1 to 1¼ lb.)**
**1 medium red pepper, cut into thin strips**
**½ pound spinach (stems removed) cut into bite-size pieces**
**1 medium carrot, shredded**

**Yield:** 4 Servings

In small bowl combine soy sauce, sherry, water, Hoisin sauce, cornstarch, sugar, ginger and garlic. Cook at **HIGH** 2½ to 3½ minutes or until thickened; stir twice. In 3-quart casserole, combine sauce and chicken. Cook at **HIGH** 4 minutes; stir twice. Add red pepper and cook at **HIGH** 2 minutes; stir once. Add spinach and carrots. Cook at **HIGH** 1 to 1½ minutes. Toss spinach with chicken mixture until spinach begins to wilt slightly. Serve immediately.

## CHICKEN PARMIGIANA

**¼ cup water**
**1 egg**
**2 boneless chicken breasts, skinned and halved**
**1 cup seasoned dry bread crumbs**
**½ cup grated Parmesan cheese**
**¼ teaspoon paprika**
**2 tablespoons oil**
**1 can (8oz.) tomato sauce or 1 cup spaghetti sauce**
**Oregano**
**1 cup (4 oz.) shredded mozzarella cheese**

**Yield:** 4 Servings

Beat egg with water. Dip chicken in bread crumbs mixed with Parmesan cheese and paprika, then in egg and again in bread crumb mixture. Coat bottom of 8-inch square dish with 1 tablespoon oil. Place chicken in dish; sprinkle with remaining oil. Cook at **HIGH** 3 to 4 minutes; turn chicken. Cook at **HIGH** 3 to 4 minutes. Top with tomato sauce and season with oregano. Cook at **HIGH** 6 to 8 minutes, or until sauce is hot. Sprinkle with mozzarella cheese and let stand, covered, 5 minutes or until cheese is melted.

## VEGETABLE-STUFFED CHICKEN BREASTS

**4 large boneless chicken breasts, skinned, split and pounded thin (about 2 lb.)**
**Salt**
**Pepper**
**1 cup frozen mixed broccoli, carrots and onions, defrosted (see page 9), finely chopped**
**2 tablespoons butter or margarine**
**½ cup flour**
**1 egg, beaten with 2 tablespoons water**
**1 cup seasoned dry bread crumbs**

**Yield:** 4 Servings

Season breasts with salt and pepper. Spoon ¼ cup of vegetables onto each breast. Top with ½ tablespoon butter, then fold edges over to enclose the filling. Secure with toothpicks. Coat chicken breasts with flour, dip in egg then in bread crumbs. Arrange chicken in 8-inch square dish. Cover with wax paper. Cook at **MEDIUM** 12 to 14 minutes, or until chicken is done.

## ORIENTAL CHICKEN AND CASHEWS

**3 tablespoons oil**
**2 boneless chicken breasts, skinned and thinly sliced (about 1 to 1¼ lb.)**
**2 cloves garlic, finely chopped**
**2 tablespoons soy sauce**
**1 tablespoon sherry**
**1 tablespoon cornstarch**
**¼ teaspoon ginger**
**1 medium green pepper, cut into small chunks**
**½ cup cashew halves or chopped walnuts**

**Yield:** 4 Servings

Heat oil in 3-quart casserole at **HIGH** 2½ to 3 minutes. Meanwhile, combine chicken, garlic, soy sauce, sherry, cornstarch and ginger. Add to dish and cook at **HIGH** 4 to 5 minutes; stir twice. Add green pepper and cashews. Cover with plastic wrap. Cook at **HIGH** 3 to 5 minutes, or until chicken and green pepper are tender; stir once. Let stand, covered, 3 minutes before serving.

## CHICKEN ENCHILADAS

**1 large onion, chopped**
**½ cup chopped green pepper**
**2 cups finely chopped cooked chicken or turkey**
**½ cup chopped ripe olives**
**2 cans (10 oz.ea.) mild enchilada sauce, divided**
**1½ cups (6 oz.) shredded Cheddar cheese, divided**
**8 corn tortillas**
**Shredded lettuce, optional**
**Sour cream, optional**

**Yield:** 4 Servings

In medium glass bowl, combine onion and green pepper. Cover with plastic wrap. Cook at **HIGH** 3 minutes; stir once. Stir in chicken, olives and ½ cup enchilada sauce. Cover with plastic wrap. Cook at **HIGH** 2 minutes, or until hot. Stir in ½ cup cheese. Let stand, covered.
Arrange two tortillas side-by-side on paper towel. Cover with another paper towel. Repeat with remaining tortillas stacking one layer on top of the other. Heat at **HIGH** 1 minute. (This softens tortillas and makes them easier to roll.) Spoon about ⅓ cup chicken filling down center of each tortilla. Roll cup tortilla and place seam-side down in 12x8-inch dish. Pour remaining sauce over tortillas. Cover with wax paper. Cook at **HIGH** 9 to 10 minutes. Top enchiladas with remaining cheese. Cook at **HIGH** 3 minutes. Let stand 3 minutes before serving. Serve garnished with lettuce and sour cream.

## CHICKEN À LA KING

**⅓ cup butter or margarine**
**2 tablespoons finely chopped green pepper**
**⅓ cup flour**
**1 teaspoon salt**
**⅛ teaspoon pepper**
**1¼ cups chicken broth**
**1¼ cups milk or half'n half**
**3 cups cut-up cooked chicken or turkey**
**1 jar (4 oz.) sliced pimento, drained (about ⅓ cup)**
**1 can (4 oz.) sliced mushrooms, drained**
**2 tablespoons dry sherry, optional**

**Yield:** 6 Servings

Combined butter and green pepper in 3-quart casserole. Cook at **HIGH** 3 to 5 minutes, or until green pepper is tender. Stir in flour, salt and pepper. Gradually add broth and milk, stir until smooth. Cook at **MEDIUM** 12 to 14 minutes, or until sauce is thickened; stir twice. Add remaining ingredients. Cook at **MEDIUM** 8 to 12 minutes, or until heated through; stir twice. Serve over toast, noodles or rice.

## CHICKEN WITH VEGETABLE STUFFING

**1 cup herb-flavored stuffing mix**
**1 cup peeled, cubed eggplant**
**1 medium green pepper, cut in chunks**
**1 medium tomato, peeled and diced**
**1 medium onion, chopped**
**1/4 cup sliced fresh mushrooms**
**1 clove garlic, finely chopped**
**2 tablespoons butter or margarine**
**1/2 teaspoon sage**
**1/2 teaspoon salt**
**1/8 teaspoon pepper**
**3 to 4 pounds whole chicken**
**Browning sauce**

**Yield:** 6 Servings

In medium glass bowl, combine stuffing mix, eggplant, green pepper, tomato, onion, mushrooms, garlic, butter, sage, salt and pepper. Cook at **HIGH** 5 to 6 minutes. Stuff chicken with vegetable mixture. With cotton string, tie legs together. Place chicken, breast-side down, on microwave roasting rack set in 8-inch square dish. Brush with browning sauce. Cover with wax paper. Cook at **MEDIUM** 27 to 36 minutes. Turn breast-side up halfway through cooking. Let stand, covered, 10 minutes before serving.

**Hint:** Halfway through cooking, shield legs and wings with aluminum foil to prevent overcooking.

## CHICKEN IN WINE SAUCE

**1 medium onion, sliced**
**1/4 cup butter or margarine**
**2 boneless chicken breasts, skinned and thinly sliced (about 1 lb.)**
**Salt and pepper to taste**
**1 medium green pepper, cut into thin strips**
**1/3 cup white wine**
**1 jar (4 1/2 oz.) sliced mushrooms, drained**
**2 tablespoons flour**
**2/3 cup chicken broth**

**Yield:** 4 Servings

Combine onion and butter in 8-inch square dish. Cook at **HIGH** 4 to 5 minutes, or until onion is tender; add chicken. Cook at **HIGH** 4 to 5 minutes; stir once. Season with salt and pepper; add green pepper and wine. Cover with plastic wrap. Cook at **HIGH** 3 to 4 minutes; add mushrooms. Blend flour with broth until smooth. Stir into dish. Cook at **HIGH** 3 to 4 minutes, or until sauce is thickened; stir twice.

## CORNISH HENS WITH PECAN STUFFING

**2 stalks celery, chopped**
**1 small onion, chopped**
**1/4 cup sliced fresh mushrooms**
**1 tablespoon butter or margarine**
**1/2 teaspoon thyme**
**1/2 teaspoon salt**
**1/8 teaspoon pepper**
**1 cup cooked long grain and wild rice (see page 30)**
**1/2 cup chopped pecans**
**2 Cornish hens (1 to 1 1/4 lb. ea.)**
**Browning sauce**

**Yield:** 4 Servings

In medium glass bowl, combine celery, onion, mushrooms, butter, thyme, salt and pepper. Cook at **HIGH** 5 to 6 minutes, or until celery and onion are tender. Add rice and pecans; combine thoroughly. Stuff hens with pecan mixture. With cotton string, tie legs together. Place hens breast-side up on microwave roasting rack set in 8-inch square dish. Brush with browning sauce. Cover with wax paper. Cook at **HIGH** 17 to 20 minutes, or until hens are tender. Let stand, covered, 5 minutes.

## TURKEY TETRAZZINI

**1/4 cup butter or margarine**
**1/4 cup flour**
**1 teaspoon salt**
**1/4 teaspoon pepper**
**1 cup chicken broth**
**1 cup half'n half**
**4 cups cut-up cooked turkey or chicken**
**1 package (8 oz.) spaghetti, cooked and drained (see page 30)**
**1 can (4 oz.) sliced mushrooms, drained**
**2 tablespoons sherry, optional**
**1/4 cup grated Parmesan cheese**
**Paprika**

**Yield:** 6 Servings

Heat butter in 3-quart casserole at **MEDIUM-LOW** 2 minutes, or until melted; stir in flour, salt, and pepper. Gradually add broth and half'n half; stir until smooth. Cook at **MEDIUM** 7 to 8 minutes, or until sauce is thickened; stir three times. Stir in turkey, spaghetti, mushrooms and sherry.
Cover with plastic wrap. Cook at **MEDIUM** 12 to 16 minutes. Stir twice. Top with Parmesan cheese and paprika. Let stand, covered, 5 minutes before serving.

## PREPARING CONVENIENCE SAUCES

- Use a glass container twice the volume of the sauce.
- Prepare sauce ingredients according to package directions
- a wire whisk is helpful in eliminating lumps when stirring dry ingredients into liquids.
- If needed, melt butter at **MEDIUM-LOW.**
- Cook sauces according to directions in chart.
- To blend flavors, when necessary, cook at **MEDIUM** or **MEDIUM-LOW.**
- Stir occasionally during heating.

| ITEM | POWER | APPROX. COOKING TIME (in minutes) |
|---|---|---|
| **Packaged Sauce** and **Gravy Mixes** (3/4 to 1 1/2 oz.) | | |
| prepared with water | HIGH | 3 to 4 |
| prepared with milk | HIGH | 3 1/2 to 8 |
| **Sauces from condensed cream-style soups** | HIGH | 6 to 7 |
| **Spaghetti Sauce Mix** (2-cup yield) | | |
| prepared with tomato sauce | HIGH, then MEDIUM-LOW | 3<br>8 to 10 |
| prepared with tomato paste | HIGH, then MEDIUM-LOW | 3<br>10 to 12 |

## BARBECUE SAUCE

**1 cup chili sauce**
**3/4 cup water**
**1/4 cup lemon juice**
**1 envelope (1 3/8 oz.) onion soup mix**
**1/2 cup packed brown sugar**
**1 teaspoon dry mustard**
**1/8 teaspoon garlic powder**

**Yield:** 2 Cups

Combine all ingredients in 1 1/2 quart bowl. Cook at **HIGH** 10 to 12 minutes or until sauce is slightly thickened; stir occasionally. Let stand 5 minutes to complete cooking onions. Use as a basting sauce on chicken, ribs, hamburgers, etc.

## BASIC WHITE SAUCE

**2 tablespoons butter or margarine**
**2 tablespoons flour**
**1/2 teaspoon salt, optional**
**Dash white pepper, optional**
**1 cup milk**

**Yield:** 1 1/4 Cups

Place butter in 4-cup glass measure. Cook at **HIGH** 20 to 30 seconds, or until melted. Stir in flour, salt and pepper. Gradually add milk; stir until smooth. Cook at **MEDIUM** 4 1/2 to 5 minutes, or until sauce is thickened; stir twice.

***Variations:***
***For CHEESE Sauce,*** *stir in 1/2 to 3/4 cup shredded cheese. Heat at* ***MEDIUM*** *1 minute, if necessary, to completely melt cheese.*

## HOMEMADE GRAVY

**1 to 2 tablespoons butter or margarine**
**2 tablespoons flour**
**Salt and pepper to taste**
**Few drops browning sauce, optional**
**1 cup roast drippings***

**Yield:** 1 Cup

Place butter in 4-cup glass measure. Cook at **HIGH** 1/2 to 1 minute, or until melted. Stir in flour, salt, pepper and browning sauce. Gradually add drippings; stir until smooth. Cook at **HIGH** 2 1/2 to 4 minutes, or until thickened; stir twice.

****Note:*** *If necessary, add broth, milk or water to roast drippings to equal 1 cup. If using milk, heat at* ***MEDIUM*** *3 to 4 minutes.*

## HOT FUDGE SAUCE

**4 squares (1 oz.ea.) unsweetened or semi-sweet chocolate**
**1 cup sugar**
**1 cup heavy cream**
**1/4 cup butter or margarine**
**1 tablespoon corn syrup**
**1 teaspoon vanilla**

**Yield:** 2 Cups

In 2-quart glass bowl, combine chocolate, sugar, cream, butter and syrup. Cook at **HIGH** 9 to 11 minutes. Mixture will boil briskly; stir three times. Cool 15 minutes; stir in vanilla until smooth. Serve.

***To reheat:*** *Heat at* ***HIGH*** *2 to 3 minutes, or until hot; stir once.*

## PREPARING CONVENIENCE SOUP MIXES

**Canned Soup:** Empty contents of can into casserole dish. Dilute according to label directions with water or milk. Cover with lid and heat according to times given in chart. Stir once. After heating, stir; let stand, covered, 2 minutes.

**Packaged Soup Mixes:** Use a casserole which is twice the volume of the water recommended on the soup mix package. Add hot tap water and soup mix to the dish; stir. Cover with lid. Bring liquid to a boil and heat according to time given in chart. Stir once. After heating, stir; let stand, covered, 2 to 3 minutes.

| SOUP | POWER | COOKING TIME (in minutes) |
|---|---|---|
| **Canned Condensed** | | |
| ($10\frac{1}{2}$ to $11\frac{1}{2}$ oz.) | | |
| with water | HIGH | 5 to 7 |
| with milk | MEDIUM | 5 to 7 |
| **Semi-Condensed,** single serving | | |
| ($7\frac{1}{2}$ to $7\frac{3}{4}$ oz.) | | |
| with water | HIGH | 3 to 4 |
| with milk | MEDIUM | 4 to 5 |
| **Ready-to-Heat** | | |
| ($10\frac{3}{4}$ to $13\frac{3}{4}$ oz.) | HIGH | 3 to 5 |
| (19 oz.) | HIGH | 5 to 6 |
| **Packaged Dry Soup Mix** | | |
| Narrow Noodles | | |
| to heat to a boil | HIGH | 5 to 8 |
| to simmer | LOW | 1 to 3 |
| Broad Noodles | | |
| to heat to a boil | HIGH | 5 to 8 |
| to simmer | LOW | 5 to 7 |

## EGG DROP SOUP

**2 cups water**
**2 green onions, sliced**
**2 envelopes chicken bouillon**
**1 egg, beaten**
**2 teaspoons chopped parsley**

**Yield:** 2 Servings

Combine water and onions in 4-cup measure. Cover with plastic wrap. Cook at **HIGH** 5 to 6 minutes, or until water boils. Stir in bouillon. Gradually pour egg into bouillon mixture; let stand 15 seconds. Stir gently with a fork to mix egg. Stir in parsley. Serve immediately.

## CREAM OF BROCCOLI SOUP

**6 tablespoons butter or margarine**
**1 tablespoon finely chopped onion**
**5 tablespoons flour**
**1 cup chicken broth**
**2 cups milk**
**$\frac{3}{4}$ teaspoon salt**
**Dash pepper**
**Dash nutmeg, optional**
**1 package (10 oz.) frozen chopped broccoli, defrosted (see page 9)**

**Yield:** 4 Servings

Combine butter and onion in 2-quart casserole. Cook at **HIGH** 2 to $2\frac{1}{2}$ minutes. Blend in flour. Gradually add broth, milk, salt, pepper and nutmeg, stir until smooth. Cook at **MEDIUM** 7 to 9 minutes, or until soup is slightly thickened; stir occasionally. Add broccoli and puree in batches in food processor or blender. Return to casserole. Cook at **MEDIUM** 3 to 4 minutes; stir once.

***Variations:***
***For Cream of MUSHROOM Soup,*** *follow above procedure. Substitute 2 cans (4 oz. ea.) sliced mushrooms, drained, for broccoli.*

***For Cream of SPINACH Soup,*** *follow above procedure. Substitute 1 package (10 oz.) frozen spinach, defrosted, for broccoli.*

## MOM'S HOMEMADE CHICKEN SOUP

**$1\frac{1}{2}$ to 2 pounds chicken parts**
**3 stalks celery, cut up**
**1 onion, sliced**
**2 bay leaves**
**$1\frac{1}{2}$ to 2 teaspoons peppercorns (or pepper) to taste**
**6 cups hot water**
**2 carrots, shredded (about 1 cup)**
**1 to $1\frac{1}{2}$ cups fine egg noodles**
**2 teaspoons salt**

**Yield:** 8 Servings

In 4-quart casserole, combine chicken, celery, onion, bay leaves, peppercorns and water. Cover with lid. Cook at **HIGH** 10 minutes and at **MEDIUM-LOW** 25 to 30 minutes, or until chicken is tender; stir twice. Remove chicken and cool. Strain broth into bowl and pour back into casserole. Add carrots, noodles and salt to broth; cover. Cook at **HIGH** 7 to 8 minutes. Meanwhile, remove chicken from bones. Add chicken to soup. Let stand, covered, 7 to 8 minutes, or until noodles are tender.

## MANHATTAN CLAM CHOWDER

**1 can (10½ oz.) condensed vegetable soup**
**1 ½ cups tomato juice or water**
**1 can (7½ oz.) minced clams**
**Dash thyme**

**Yield:** 4 Servings

Combine all ingredients in 1½-quart casserole. Cover with lid. Cook at **HIGH** 8 to 11 minutes; stir occasionally.
Let stand, covered, 3 minutes. Serve, if desired, with oyster crackers.

## FRENCH ONION SOUP

**3 tablespoons butter or margarine**
**3 cups sliced onions (about 3 medium)**
**2 cans (10½ oz. ea.) condensed beef broth**
**1½ cups water**
**1 teaspoon Worcestershire sauce**
**Salt and pepper to taste**
**Croutons**
**Grated Parmesan cheese**

**Yield:** 4 Servings

Place butter and onions in 3-quart casserole. Cover with lid. Cook at **HIGH** 7 to 10 minutes, or until onions are tender; stir twice.
Stir in broth, water, Worcestershire sauce, salt and pepper; cover. Cook at **HIGH** 9 to 10 minutes. Serve with croutons and Parmesan cheese.

## SAVORY SPLIT PEA SOUP

**½ pound bacon, diced**
**6 cups hot water**
**1 package (16 oz.) dried split peas**
**5 stalks celery, chopped**
**1 medium onion, chopped**
**3 carrots, sliced**
**1 teaspoon salt**
**⅛ teaspoon thyme or basil, optional**
**Pepper to taste**

**Yield:** 6 Servings

Place bacon in 4-quart casserole. Cook at **HIGH** 8 to 9 minutes; stir once. Add remaining ingredients. Cover with lid. Cook at **HIGH** 12 minutes and at **MEDIUM** 45 to 50 minutes or until peas are tender; stir occasionally.
Put mixture through food mill or puree in food processor or blender. Reheat, adding additonal water, if necessary, at **MEDIUM** 4 to 6 minutes.

## MINESTRONE

**2 tablespoons butter or margarine**
**3 carrots, thinly sliced**
**1 medium onion, chopped**
**2 cups chicken broth**
**1 can (16 oz.) stewed tomatoes, chopped**
**1 cup shredded cabbage or zucchini**
**1 teaspoon basil**
**1 teaspoon parsley flakes**
**1 teaspoon salt**
**1 can (19 oz.) kidney beans, drained**
**¼ to ⅓ cup broken spaghetti (about 2-inch pieces)**

**Yield:** 4 Servings

In 3-quart casserole, combine butter, carrots and onions. Cover with lid. Cook at **HIGH** 5 to 7 minutes. Add broth, tomatoes, cabbage, basil, parsley and salt. Cook, covered, at **HIGH** 7 to 9 minutes; stir once. Add kidney beans and spaghetti. Cook, covered, at **MEDIUM** 13 to 15 minutes, or until spaghetti is tender; stir once. Let stand, covered, 5 minutes.

## VICHYSSOISE

**3 tablespoons butter or margarine**
**3 medium leeks, white part, sliced**
**1½ cups chicken broth**
**¾ teaspoon salt**
**⅛ teaspoon pepper**
**2 medium potatoes, baked (see page 41)**
**1½ cup milk**
**1 cup heavy cream**
**1 tablesppon sherry, optional**
**Chopped chives**

**Yield:** 4 Servings

Combine butter and leeks in 2-quart casserole. Cook at **HIGH** 3 to 5 minutes; stir in broth, salt and pepper. Cook, covered with lid, at **HIGH** 3 to 5 minutes and at **MEDIUM** 6 minutes.
Meanwhile, peel and dice potatoes. With electric mixer, blender or food processor puree potatoes, broth mixture and milk. Return to dish. Reheat, covered, at **MEDIUM** 3 to 4 minutes; stir in cream and sherry.
Chill thoroughly and garnish, if desired, with chopped chives before serving.

## DIRECTIONS FOR COOKING FROZEN VEGETABLES

**Frozen Vegetables**
For 9 to 10-ounce packages, remove vegetables from their package and place in 1 or 1½-quart casserole. Add 2 tablespoons water to frozen artichokes, Brussels sprouts, sliced and whole okra and ½ cup water plus 1 tablespoon butter or margarine to frozen lima beans. Cover with lid. Cook at **HIGH** 5 to 9 minutes or until slightly tender. Stir halfway through cooking. Let stand, covered, 3 minutes before serving.

**Frozen Vegetables in a Pouch**
Remove pouch from package, place on a microwave safe plate. Cut small slit in center of pouch. Cook at **HIGH,** following times on package directions (approximately 3¾ to 7 minutes, depending on vegetable). Let stand 2 minutes before serving.

**Frozen Corn on the Cob**
Rinse off any frost. Place frozen corn in a square dish. Cover with plastic wrap. Cook at **HIGH.** Rearrange and turn corn over halfway through cooking. Let stand, covered, 3 to 5 minutes before serving. Cook at **HIGH** as follows:
1 ear: 4 to 5½ min. 2 ears: 6½ to 8½ min.
3 ear: 9 to 11 min. 4 ears: 12 to 14 min.

## DIRECTIONS FOR COOKING FRESH VEGETABLES

Weights given in the chart for fresh vegetables are the purchase weights before peeling and trimming.

Prepare vegetables for cooking. Cut into size recommended in chart.

Place vegetables in casserole. Add amount of water recommended in chart. Add salt to water or salt after cooking. Cover with lid or plastic wrap.

Whole vegetables, such as potatoes or eggplant should be pierced with a fork several times before cooking. Arrange on a paper towel in oven. Arrange potatoes in a circular pattern on paper towel.

Cook according to time recommended in chart. Two-thirds the way through cooking, stir, rearrange and/or turn vegetables over. Let stand, covered, before serving. Whole vegetables should stand 5 minutes. Vegetables that are cut into pieces should stand 3 minutes.

## FRESH VEGETABLE CHART

| VEGETABLE | AMOUNT | WATER | APPROX. COOKING TIME AT HIGH (in minutes) |
|---|---|---|---|
| **Artichokes,** 6 to 8 oz. ea. | 1<br>2<br>4 | 1 tablespoon<br>2 tablespoons<br>¼ cup | 6 to 7<br>8½ to 10<br>12½ to 14 |
| **Asparagus,** 6-in. spears | 1 lb. | 2 tablespoons | 5 to 6 |
| **Beans,** Green or Wax, cut into 1½-in. pieces | 1 lb. | ¼ cup | 7½ to 8½ |
| **Broccoli,** cut into spears | 1 lb. | ¼ cup | 6 to 7 |
| **Brussels Sprouts** | 1 tub (10 oz.) | 2 tablespoons | 5½ to 7 |
| **Cabbage,** shredded | 4 cups | ¼ cup | 6½ to 8 |
| **Carrots,** sliced ½-in. thick | 1 lb. | ¼ cup | 7 to 8½ |
| **Corn,** on the Cob | 1 ear<br>2 ears<br>4 ears | 2 tablespoons<br>2 tablespoons<br>¼ cup | 3 to 3½<br>4 to 4½<br>10 to 10½ |
| **Eggplant,** cubed<br>whole (pierce skin) | 1 lb.<br>1 to 1¼ lb. | ¼ cup<br>— | 7 to 8½<br>4½ to 6 |
| **Onions,** small whole | 8 to 10 (1 lb.) | ¼ cup | 6½ to 8 |
| **Peas,** Green | 1½ lb. | ¼ cup | 5 to 6½ |
| **Potatoes,** about 8 oz. ea: Turn over halfway through cooking. | 1<br>2<br>4 | —<br>—<br>— | 4½ to 5½<br>7 to 9<br>12 to 14 |
| **Spinach,** leaf | 1 lb. | — | 5½ to 6½ |
| **Squash, Summer,** sliced ½-in. thick | 1 lb. | ¼ cup | 6½ to 8 |
| **Squash, Winter,** whole, about 1 lb. ea., cut in half | 1 | ¼ cup | 6½ to 7 |

## CLASSIC COMPANY GREEN BEANS

**2 packages (9 oz. ea.) frozen French-style green beans**
**1 can (10¾ oz.) condensed cream of mushroom soup**
**1 can (3 oz.) French fried onions**

**Yield:** 6 Servings

Place beans in 2-quart casserole. Cover with lid. Cook at **HIGH** 9 to 11 minutes, or until beans are tender; stir twice. Stir in soup and half of onion pieces; top with remaining onion pieces. Cook at **HIGH** 6 to 8 minutes. Let stand 3 minutes before serving.

## SESAME, BROCCOLI AND CAULIFLOWER

**3 tablespoons oil**
**1 tablespoon toasted sesame seeds (see page 48)**
**½ bunch broccoli, cut into flowerets**
**1 small head cauliflower, cut into flowerets**
**1 tablespoon soy sauce**
**¼ teaspoon ginger**

**Yield:** 4 Servings

Place oil and sesame seeds in 3-quart casserole. Cook at **HIGH** 4 minutes. Add broccoli and cauliflower. Mix soy sauce and ginger. Pour over vegetables; stir well. Cover with plastic wrap. Cook at **HIGH** 6 to 8 minutes; stir once.

## ORANGE GLAZED CARROTS

**¼ cup orange juice**
**3 tablespoons honey**
**3 tablespoons butter or margarine, melted**
**½ teaspoon grated lemon peel, optional**
**¼ teaspoon salt**
**Dash nutmeg**
**2 teaspoons cornstarch**
**1 pound carrots, sliced ½-inch thick**

**Yield:** 4 Servings

In 2-quart casserole, combine juice, honey, butter, lemon peel, salt and nutmeg. Stir in cornstarch; mix until well blended. Stir in carrots. Cover with lid. Cook at **HIGH** 7 to 9 minutes; stir once. Stir; let stand, covered, 3 minutes before serving.

## HONEY ACORN SQUASH

**2 acorn squash (about ¾ lb. ea.)**
**4 tablespoons honey**
**4 teaspoons butter or margarine**
**⅛ teaspoon grated lemon peel**

**Yield:** 4 Servings

Pierce skin of squash several times, arrange on paper towel-lined glass oven tray. Cook at **HIGH** 4 to 5 minutes, turning squash over once; let stand 3 minutes. Cut squash in half; scoop out seeds. Arrange squash, cut-side up, in 10-inch square dish. Top with honey, butter and lemon. Cover with plastic wrap. Cook at **HIGH** 5 to 6 minutes, or until squash is tender. Let stand, covered, 2 minutes before serving.

***Variations:*** *Use one of the following toppings for honey, butter and lemon —* ***For FRUIT 'N HONEY SQUASH,*** *use 4 tablespoons finely chopped apple, 2 tablespoons flaked coconut, 4 tablespoons honey and 2 tablespoons butter.*

***For HOLIDAY SPECIAL SQUASH,*** *use ½ cup chopped orange, ¼ cup whole berry cranberry sauce, 2 tablespoons packed brown sugar and ¼ teaspoon cinnamon.*

## SWISS SCALLOPED CORN

**3 slices bacon, crisp-cooked and crumbled (see page 23)**
**2 cans (17 oz. ea.) whole kernel corn, drained**
**1 cup (4 oz.) shredded Swiss cheese**
**1 egg**
**1 can (5⅓ oz.) evaporated milk**
**½ teaspoon onion powder**
**⅛ teaspoon pepper**
**1½ tablespoons flour**
**¼ cup dry bread crumbs**
**1 tablespoon butter or margarine, melted**
**Paprika**

**Yield:** 6 servings

In 12x8-inch dish, combine bacon, corn, and cheese. Blend in egg, milk, onion powder, pepper, and flour. Cook at **MEDIUM** 5 to 6 minutes; stir once. Combine bread crumbs, butter and paprika. Sprinkle over corn. Cover with plastic wrap. Cook at **MEDIUM** 10 to 13 minutes. Let stand, uncovered, 5 minutes before serving.

## GREEN BEANS AMANDINE

**1/4 cup slivered almonds**
**3 tablespoons butter or margarine**
**1 1/4 to 1 1/2 pounds fresh green beans, cut into 1 1/2-inch pieces**
**1/4 cup water**
**1/2 teaspoon salt**
**Dash ground nutmeg, optional**

**Yield:** 4 Servings

Combine almonds and butter in 2-cup glass measure. Cook at **HIGH** 3 to 4 minutes, or until almonds are lightly browned; reserve. Combine beans and water in 2-quart casserole. Cover with lid. Cook at **HIGH** 9 to 12 minutes, or until beans are tender; stir once. Drain. Add remaining ingredients, almonds and butter; let stand, covered, 3 minutes before serving.

## WILTED GREENS

**3 slices bacon, diced**
**1 small onion, chopped**
**1/4 cup white wine vinegar**
**1 tablespoon prepared mustard**
**1/2 teaspoon horseradish**
**1/2 teaspoon salt**
**Dash pepper**
**1 pound greens (leafy lettuce, escarole or spinach) cut into bite-size pieces, about 6 cups firmly packed.**

**Yield:** 4 Servings

Place bacon and onion in 3-quart casserole. Cover with lid. Cook at **HIGH** 6 to 6 1/2 minutes, or until bacon is lightly browned. Add vinegar, sugar, mustard, horseradish, salt and pepper; stir. Add greens; toss well. Cover. Cook at **HIGH** 2 to 3 minutes, or until greens are wilted.

## HERB-BAKED TOMATOES

**3 tablespoons seasoned dry bread crumbs**
**2 tablespoons butter or margarine, melted**
**2 tablespoons grated Parmesan cheese**
**1/2 teaspoon oregano or basil**
**2 medium tomatoes, cut in half**

**Yield:** 4 Servings

Combine bread crumbs, butter, cheese and oregano.
Arrange tomato halves in 8-inch square dish; top with bread crumb mixture. Cover with plastic wrap. Cook at **HIGH** 2 to 2 1/2 minutes or until tomatoes are tender. Let stand 2 minutes before serving.

## SCALLOPED POTATOES

**1/4 cup butter or margarine**
**1 tablespoon dried onion flakes**
**1 teaspoon salt**
**1/4 teaspoon pepper**
**1/4 cup flour**
**2 cups milk**
**6 medium potatoes (about 6 oz. ea.), peeled and thinly sliced**

**Yield:** 6 Servings

In 4-cup glass measure, combine butter, onion, salt and pepper. Cook at **HIGH** 1 to 1 1/2 minutes, or until butter is melted. Stir in flour; gradually add milk, stirring until smooth. Cook at **MEDIUM** 8 to 9 minutes, or until sauce is thickened; stir twice. In 2-quart casserole, alternately layer potatoes and sauce, forming three layers. Cover with plastic wrap. Cook at **MEDIUM** 27 to 30 minutes, or until potatoes are tender. Let stand, covered, 5 minutes.

## BAKED STUFFED POTATOES

**4 medium potatoes, baked (see page 41)**
**1/2 cup (2 oz.) shredded Cheddar cheese**
**1/3 to 1/2 cup milk**
**2 tablespoons butter or margarine, softened**
**1 egg**
**Salt and pepper to taste**
**Paprika**

**Yield:** 4 Servings

Cut a thin slice (lengthwise) from each potato. Scoop out potato leaving a thin shell. In small bowl, combine potato, cheese, milk, butter egg, salt and pepper; mash until smooth. Spoon potato mixture into shell; sprinkle with paprika. In 8-inch square dish, arrange potatoes in a circle. Cover with wax paper. Cook at **MEDIUM** 4 to 6 minutes. Let stand, uncovered, 3 minutes before serving.

***Note: For TWO Servings,*** *follow above procedure; halve all ingredients (use whole egg). Cook 2 to 3 minutes.*

## MASHED POTATOES

**6 medium potatoes (about 2 pounds), peeled and quartered**
**1/2 to 3/4 cup milk**
**1/4 cup butter or margarine**
**Salt and pepper to taste**

**Yield:** 6 Servings

Rinse potatoes; drain. Arrange potatoes in medium glass bowl. Cover with plastic wrap. Cook at **HIGH** 13 to 15 minutes; stir once. Potatoes should be tender. Let stand, covered, 5 minutes. Drain. Meanwhile, in large glass bowl, combine remaining ingredients; cook at **MEDIUM** 3 to 4 minutes, or until hot. Add potatoes and mash until smooth.

***Note: For INSTANT Mashed Potatoes,*** *follow package directions; cook water, milk and salt in bowl at* ***HIGH****. Stir in butter and instant potato flakes.*

## COMPANY PEAS

**2 packages (10 oz. ea.) frozen peas**
**1/2 cup sliced green onions**
**1 package (19 oz.) instant chicken broth**
**2 teaspoons chopped fresh mint**
**Dash pepper**
**1/4 head lettuce, finely shredded**

**Yield:** 6 Servings

In 3-quart casserole, combine peas, onions, chicken broth, mint and pepper. Cover with lid. Cook at **HIGH** 8 to 9 minutes. Stir twice. Add lettuce. Cover. Cook at **HIGH** 3 to 4 minutes. Stir once. Let stand, covered, 3 minutes before serving.

## DEVILED MUSHROOMS

**2 tablespoons butter or margarine**
**2 tablespoons dry vermouth or sherry**
**1 tablespoon Dijon-style mustard or spicy brown mustard**
**2 teaspoons cornstarch**
**1/4 to 1/2 teaspoon salt**
**1/8 teaspoon pepper**
**12 ounces mushrooms, sliced**

**Yield:** 4—6 Servings

Place butter in 2-quart casserole. Cook at **HIGH** 1 to 1 1/4 minutes, or until melted. Stir in wine, mustard, cornstarch, salt and pepper until smooth. Add mushrooms; cover with lid. Cook at **HIGH** 5 1/2 to 6 1/2 minutes, or until mushrooms are tender and sauce is thickened; stir twice.

## RATATOUILLE

**1 medium onion, sliced**
**1 small green pepper, cut into 1/2-inch slices**
**1/3 cup oil**
**1 clove garlic, finely chopped**
**1 small eggplant, peeled and cut into 3/4-inch pieces**
**2 medium tomatoes, cut into eighths**
**1 medium zucchini, cut into 1/2-inch slices**
**1/4 cup vegetable juice cocktail or tomato juice**
**1 teaspoon each basil and parsley flakes**
**1/2 teaspoon salt**
**1/4 teaspoon pepper**

**Yield:** 8 Servings

In 3-quart casserole combine onion, green pepper, oil and garlic. Cover with lid. Cook at **HIGH** 4 to 5 minutes; stir once. Stir in remaining ingredients; cover. Cook at **HIGH** 18 to 20 minutes; stir twice. Let stand, covered, 5 minutes before serving.

***Variation:*** *Add 1/4 pound fresh mushrooms, sliced or 1 can (4 oz.) sliced mushrooms, drained, with eggplant.*

## ZUCCHINI BOATS

**2 medium zucchini (about 1 1/4 lb.)**
**1 clove garlic, finely chopped**
**1 medium onion, chopped**
**1 stalk celery, chopped**
**3/4 teaspoon basil**
**1/4 teaspoon oregano**
**1/4 teaspoon salt**
**Dash pepper**
**1 can (8 oz.) whole tomatoes, drained and chopped**
**1/4 cup dry bread crumbs**
**4 tablespoons grated Parmesan cheese, divided**

**Yield:** 4 Servings

Cut zucchini in half lengthwise and scoop out centers; chop centers. In medium glass bowl, combine chopped zucchini, garlic, onion, celery, basil, oregano, salt and pepper. Cook at **HIGH** 3 1/2 to 4 minutes. Drain. Add tomatoes, bread crumbs and 3 tablespoons cheese. Spoon into zucchini shells. Place shells in 8-inch square dish. Cover with wax paper. Cook at **HIGH** 7 1/2 to 8 1/2 minutes. Sprinkle with remaining cheese. Let stand, covered, 3 minutes before serving.

## DIRECTIONS FOR QUICK BREADS AND CAKES

Layer cakes must be baked one layer at a time. Or, the entire cake mix may be baked in a 16-cup fluted tube dish.

Prepare batter according to package, chart or recipe directions.

Use dishes recommended in chart or recipes. Glass dishes allow the bottom of the cakes to be checked for doneness. When the product is removed from the oven, visually check bottom.

If cake is to be inverted or removed from dish, such as layer cakes or upside-down cakes, line bottom of 8 or 9-inch round or square dish with wax paper.

If cake is to be served directly from the dish, do not line, grease or flour dish.

Never flour cake dishes, fluted tube dishes or muffin pans.

Use only 2¼ cups of batter for an 8 or 9-inch round or square dish. Cover with wax paper. Cook second layer immediately after the first. The remaining batter can be used for cupcakes.

When using a fluted tube dish, be sure to grease sides and "tube". All the batter from a 2 layer cake mix may be poured into a 16-cup fluted tube dish.

When cooking cupcakes or muffins, line microwave muffin pans with paper baking cups. Fill paper baking cups two-thirds.

Cover with wax paper when indicated in chart or recipe.

Check during cooking. Different brands vary in ingredients and density of batter; cooking times may be slightly different than those given in chart.

After cooking, test for doneness. Check to make sure edges of cake are dry and have begun to pull away from sides of dish, and toothpick inserted near center comes out clean.

Let stand, uncovered, on a flat surface for 10 to 15 minutes. Stand time is important to allow cakes and cupcakes to finish baking.

Cakes and breads that are to be inverted should be loosened from the sides of the dish. Carefully turn out of dish. Remove wax paper from bottom of cake.

Store, covered, until ready to serve.

Frost, if desired, when completely cooled. Microwave cakes are very tender and may tear if too much pressure is applied when they are frosted.

## QUICK BREADS AND CAKE MIX CHART

| ITEM | AMOUNT OF BATTER | PREPARATION DISH SIZE | FIRST STAGE | SECOND STAGE | SPECIAL INSTRUCTIONS | STAND TIME |
|---|---|---|---|---|---|---|
| **Quick Bread** (15.4 to 17 oz.) | All batter | Line bottom of 9x5x3-inch loaf dish with wax paper | **LOW** 8 minutes | **HIGH** 5 to 6 minutes | • Shield ends with 3-inch strip of foil. Mold foil around handles. • ROTATE dish ¼ turn after 1st stage of cooking. | 15 minutes uncovered |
| **Cornbread** (8 to 10 oz.) | All batter | Grease 8 or 9-inch round or square dish | **MEDIUM** 6 to 7 minutes | — | • Rotate dish 1/4 turn halfway through cooking. | 10 minutes uncovered |
| **Gingerbread** (14 oz.) | All batter | 8-inch square dish | **MEDIUM** 9 to 10 minutes | — | • Rotate dish 1/2 turn halfway through cooking. | 15 minutes uncovered |
| **Muffins** (cook 6 at a time) | Scant ¼ cup per muffin | 6-cup muffin pan lined with paper baking cups | **MEDIUM-LOW** 4 to 5 minutes | — | • Cover with wax paper. | 5 minutes uncovered |
| **Cake Mix** (18 to 20¼ oz.) | 2¼ cups | Grease bottom of 8 or 9-inch round or square glass baking dish | **LOW** 6 minutes | **HIGH** 1½ to 2½ | • Cover with sheet of wax paper. • Rotate dish 1/4 turn after 1st stage of cooking. | 10 minutes uncovered |
| **Cake Mix** (18 to 20¼ oz.) | Prepare batter according to package directions, using only 1 cup water. Pour all batter into pan. | Grease 16-cup fluted tube dish | **MEDIUM-LOW** 14 to 15 minutes | — | • Cover pan with wax paper. • Place dish on microwave rack. • Rotate dish ¼ turn twice during cooking. • Cover with wax paper | 15 minutes uncovered 15 minutes on rack, then remove |
| **Brownies** (14.1 to 15 oz.) | All batter | Grease 8 or 9-inch round or square glass baking dish | **LOW** 6 minutes | **MEDIUM** 5 to 6 minutes | • Rotate dish ¼ turn after 1st stage of cooking. • Check bottom of brownie for uncooked batter & bake longer. | Uncovered until cool |
| **Cupcakes** | Fill cups ⅔ full | Muffin pan lined with paper baking cups<br>1<br>2<br>4<br>6 | **MEDIUM-LOW** in minutes<br>¾ to 1<br>1 to 1¼<br>1½ to 2*<br>3 to 4* | — | *Cover with wax paper during baking. | 10 minutes uncovered |

## SOUR CREAM COFFEE CAKE

**1/2 cup sugar**
**1/4 cup butter**
**1 1/2 cups flour**
**1 cup sour cream**
**2 eggs**
**1 1/2 teaspoons vanilla**
**1 teaspoon baking powder**
**1 teaspoon baking soda**
**1/2 teaspoon salt**

**Topping:**
**1/3 cup chopped walnuts**
**1/4 cup sugar**
**1/2 teaspoon cinnamon**

**Yield:** 8 Servings

In large bowl, with electric mixer, cream sugar and butter. Add remaining ingredients. Beat at low speed 30 seconds and at medium speed 2 minutes. Pour into greased 8-inch square dish. In small bowl, combine topping ingredients; sprinkle over batter. Cover with wax paper. Elevate on flat rack. Cook at **MEDIUM-LOW** 6 minutes and at **HIGH** 5 to 6 minutes, or until edges are dry and toothpick inserted near center comes out clean. Let stand, uncovered, 10 minutes. Serve immediately.

## RAISIN BRAN MUFFINS

**2/3 cup milk**
**1/3 cup oil**
**2 eggs**
**2 1/4 cups raisin bran cereal**
**2/3 cup flour**
**1/3 cup packed brown sugar**
**1 tablespoon baking powder**
**1/2 teaspoon cinnamon**

**Yield:** 12 Muffins

Combine milk, oil and eggs. Stir in cereal until moistened. Let stand 5 minutes. Combine flour, sugar, baking powder and cinnamon. Add to cereal mixture; stir until well blended . Line 6-cup muffin pan with paper baking cups; fill 2/3 full. Cook at **MEDIUM-LOW** 4 1/2 to 5 minutes, or until toothpick inserted near center comes out clean. Let stand 5 minutes. Repeat procedure with remaining batter. Serve warm.

## BANANA NUT COFFEE CAKE

**1/4 cup oil**
**1/4 cup milk**
**1 egg**
**1 mashed ripe banana**
**1/2 cup packed brown sugar**
**3/4 cup flour**
**1/2 cup chopped nuts**
**3/4 teaspoon baking powder**
**1/4 teaspoon salt**
**1/4 teaspoon baking soda**

**Nut topping:**
**1/4 cup packed brown sugar**
**1/4 cup chopped nuts**
**2 tablespoons flour**
**1/8 teaspoon cinnamon**
**1 tablespoon butter or margarine, softened**

**Yield:** 8 Servings

In medium bowl, combine oil, milk, egg, banana and sugar. Add flour, nuts, baking powder, salt and baking soda; stir only until flour is moistened. Pour into greased 8 or 9-inch round dish. In small bowl, prepare nut topping. Combine brown sugar, nuts, flour, and cinnamon; cut in butter. Sprinkle over batter. Cover with wax paper. Cook at **LOW** 6 minutes. Rotate dish 1/4 turn. Cook at **HIGH** 4 1/2 to 5 1/2 minutes, or until top is dry around edges and until toothpick inserted near center comes out clean. Let stand, uncovered, 10 minutes. Store, covered, until ready to serve.

## SOUTHERN CHEESE SPOON BREAD

**1/2 cup yellow cornmeal**
**2 cups milk**
**1/2 teaspoon salt**
**2 eggs, beaten**
**1 cup (4 oz.) diced American cheese**
**2 tablespoons butter or margarine**

**Yield:** 6 Servings

In medium glass bowl, combine cornmeal, milk and salt. Cook at **HIGH** 3 minutes and at **MEDIUM** 3 to 4 minutes, or until cornmeal is thickened; stir twice. Stir until smooth; add eggs, cheese and butter. Stir until cheese and butter are almost melted. Pour into greased 1-quart casserole dish. Cover with lid. Cook at **MEDIUM** 7 to 9 minutes, or until center is almost set. Let stand 10 minutes before serving.

## YELLOW CAKE

**3/4 cup sugar**
**1/3 cup butter or margarine**
**1 egg**
**2/3 cup milk**
**1 teaspoon vanilla**
**1 cup flour**
**1 1/2 teaspoons baking powder**
**1/4 teaspoon salt**

**Yield:** 1 Layer

Cream sugar and butter in small bowl, with electric mixer. Add egg, milk and vanilla, mixing until blended. Stir in remaining ingredients. Beat 1 minute at medium speed. Line an 8 or 9-inch round baking dish with wax paper. Pour batter into dish; cover with wax paper. Cook at **MEDIUM-LOW** 6 minutes. Rotate dish 1/4 turn. Cook at **HIGH** 2 to 3 minutes, or until toothpick inserted near center comes out clean and edges begin to pull away from sides of dish. Let stand, uncovered, 10 minutes. Invert on serving plate; peel off wax paper. Store covered.

## PINEAPPLE UPSIDE-DOWN CAKE

**6 tablespoons butter or margarine**
**1 cup packed brown sugar**
**Water**
**1 can (20 oz.) sliced pineapple, drained (reserve syrup)**
**10 maraschino cherries**
**1 package (18 1/4 oz.) yellow cake mix**
**Ingredients as cake package directs**

**Yield:** 2 Layers

Heat butter, brown sugar and 2 tablespoons water in small glass bowl at **HIGH** 4 to 5 minutes, or until mixture boils 1 minute. In 2 (8 or 9-inch) round baking dishes, spread sugar-butter mixture; arrange pineapple and cherries. Prepare cake mix according to package directions, using reserved syrup as part of water. Pour 2 cups of butter into each dish. Cover with wax paper. Cook at **LOW** 6 minutes. Rotate dish 1/4 turn. Cook at **HIGH** 3 to 3 1/2 minutes, or until toothpick inserted near center comes out clean. Let stand 10 minutes. Repeat with remaining layer. With knife, loosen cake from sides of dish, invert onto serving platter. Store covered.

## CARROT SPICE CAKE

**1 1/4 cups flour**
**1 cup packed brown sugar**
**1 teaspoon baking powder**
**1 teaspoon baking soda**
**2 teaspoons cinnamon**
**1/2 teaspoon allspice**
**1/2 teaspoon salt**
**1 1/4 cups shredded carrot**
**2/3 cup oil**
**2 eggs**
**1 can (8oz.) crushed pineapple, drained**
**1 teaspoon vanilla**
**1/2 cup chopped nuts**
**1/4 cup raisins**

**Yield:** 8 Servings

In large bowl, with electric mixer, combine flour, sugar, baking powder, baking soda, cinnamon, allspice, salt and carrot. Stir in oil, eggs, pineapple and vanilla and beat 2 minutes at medium speed. Stir in nuts and raisins. Pour batter into a greased 10 to 12 cup fluted tube dish. Cover with wax paper. Cook at **LOW** 10 minutes. Rotate dish 1/4 turn. Cook at **MEDIUM** 6 to 7 minutes, or until toothpick inserted near center comes out clean and edges begin to pull away from side of pan. Stand, uncovered, 10 minutes. Store, covered, until ready to serve.

## DEVIL'S FOOD CAKE

**3/4 cup sugar**
**1/3 cup shortening**
**1 egg**
**2/3 cup hot water**
**3/4 cup flour**
**1/4 cup unsweetened cocoa**
**1/2 teaspoon baking soda**
**1/2 teaspoon salt**
**1/2 teaspoon vanilla**
**1/4 teaspoon baking powder**

**Yield:** 1 Layer

Cream sugar and shortening in small bowl with electric mixer. Add egg and water. Stir in remaining ingredients and blend until smooth. Pour batter into 8 or 9-inch round dish, bottom lined with wax paper. Cover with wax paper. Cook at **MEDIUM-LOW** 6 minutes. Rotate dish 1/4 turn. Cook at **HIGH** 1 to 2 minutes, or until toothpick inserted near center comes out clean, and edges begin to pull away from sides of dish. Let stand 10 minutes. Invert cake from dish and cool completely. Store covered.

| FOOD | POWER | TIME (in minutes) | DIRECTIONS |
|---|---|---|---|
| **Butter, Melted,** 1/4 pound<br>**Butter, Softened,** 1/4 pound | **MEDIUM-LOW**<br>**LOW** | 1 to 2<br>1/4 to 1/2 | Remove wrapper and place butter in dish. |
| **Chocolate, Melted,** 1 square (1 oz.)<br>**Chocolate, Melted,** 1/2 cup chips | **MEDIUM-LOW**<br>**MEDIUM-LOW** | 2 to 3<br>2 to 3 | Remove wrapper and place chocolate in dish. Stir before adding more time. Chocolate holds it shape even when softened. |
| **Baby Bottle, Warmed,** 8 oz. formula or milk | **MEDIUM** | 3/4 to 1 | Remove cap and nipple. After heating, screw nipple on bottle and gently shake. Stand 1 to 2 minutes before using. Do not heat bottles with disposable linings in microwave oven. |
| **Bacon, Separated,** 1 lb. | **HIGH** | 1/4 to 1/2 | Remove wrapper. After heating, use a plastic spatula to separate slices. |
| **Cream Cheese, Softened,** 3 oz. | **LOW** | 1/2 to 1 | Remove wrapper and place in a bowl. |
| **Cup of Water**<br>1 cup (8 oz.)<br>2 cups (16 oz.)<br>**Cup of milk**<br>1 cup (8 oz.)<br>2 cups (16 oz.) | <br>**HIGH**<br>**HIGH**<br><br>**MEDIUM**<br>**MEDIUM** | <br>4<br>6 1/2<br><br>3 1/2 to 4 1/2<br>7 to 8 | Heated liquids can erupt if not mixed with air. Do not heat liquids in your microwave oven without stirring first. |
| **Coconut, Toasted,** 1/3 cup | **HIGH** | 2 to 3 | Place in a pie plate or bowl. Stir every 30 seconds. |
| **Remove Oven Odors** | **HIGH** | 5 | Combine 1 cup water with juice and peel of one lemon. After heating, wipe interior with damp cloth. |
| **Ice Cream, Softened,** 1/2 gallon | **LOW** | 3 to 4 | ——— |
| **Nuts, Roasted,** 1 1/2 cups | **HIGH** | 4 1/2 to 5 | Spread nuts in 9-inch pie plate. Stir twice. |
| **Sesame Seeds, Toasted,** 1/4 cup | **HIGH** | 3 to 4 | Place in a small bowl. Stir twice. |



Printed in Japan
(4000AQ) 87.6.⑳-2